Your UDL Journey

A Systems Approach to Transforming Instruction

Patti Kelly Ralabate

Elizabeth Berquist

Bulk discounts available: For details, email *publishing@cast.org* or visit *www.castpublishing.org*.

Copyright © 2020 by CAST, Inc. All rights reserved.

No part of this publication may be reproduced or transmitted in any form or by any means, electronic or mechanical, including photocopy, recording, or any information storage and retrieval systems, without permission in writing from the publisher.

Library of Congress Control Number: 2019955668

Paperback ISBN 978-1-930583-28-3
Ebook ISBN 978-1-930583-30-6

Published by:
CAST Professional Publishing
an imprint of CAST, Inc.
Wakefield, Massachusetts, USA

Cover and interior design by Happenstance Type-O-Rama
Cover image by mgordeev | istockphoto.com
Illustrations by Eli Brophy, Philadelphia, PA, unless otherwise noted. This includes the "Watch for UDL" image found throughout the book. The illustrator retains copyright to his works, which are used here with permission.

Printed in the United States of America

*To our families for their
enduring love and support*

CONTENTS

SECTION I: TRANSFORMING INSTRUCTION

    Chapter 1: Why Is UDL a Transformative Framework? 3

    Chapter 2: How Do We Get Started? 17

    Chapter 3: What Is the UDL Implementation Process? 31

SECTION II: IMPLEMENTATION FROM EXPLORE TO OPTIMIZE

    Chapter 4: Explore 51

    Chapter 5: Prepare 67

    Chapter 6: Integrate 89

    Chapter 7: Scale 117

    Chapter 8: Optimize 137

    Chapter 9: Beyond Implementation 155

Resources 163

References 183

Index 195

About the Authors 203

PREFACE

It is fitting that we chose the title of this book to reflect that implementing Universal Design for Learning (UDL) is a journey. The Merriam-Webster dictionary defines the word *journey* as "something suggesting travel or passage from one place to another." At a systems level, UDL implementation is akin to a personal passage from one understanding of learning and instruction to another. It is more than applying a new idea or structure to your practice. At its core, and when it is most effective, it is transformative in nature. Once you've arrived at your new destination—optimizing expert learning—you'll understand your practice with enlightened clarity through a UDL lens.

OUR JOURNEYS

From Patti Kelly Ralabate: My UDL journey started when I was introduced to the UDL framework by Fran Smith during a graduate class at the George Washington University in Washington, DC. That first step led me to explore UDL as a conceptual framework. Subsequently, while I was working at the National Education Association (NEA) as a senior policy analyst, I attended a national forum led by David Rose, one of UDL's chief architects. After decades of working on initiatives that aimed to increase inclusiveness in public schools across the country, UDL presented me with a powerful opportunity to transform instruction and learning environments for *all* learners. Intrigued, I began to investigate policies related to UDL implementation and joined Ricki Sabia and other national education advocates to create the National UDL Task Force. Through collaborative efforts, we successfully urged Congress and the US Department of Education to include the definition of UDL as an effective approach for optimizing learning in federal policy. As my journey continued, I was thrilled to have the chance, as CAST's Director of Implementation, to connect the process of implementing UDL with the systems change focus of my doctoral dissertation.

It soon became clear that resources to assist educators embarking on their own UDL journeys were hard to find. CAST created many with the support of a grant from the Bill and Melinda Gates Foundation and the perceptive insights of UDL implementation pioneers, particularly Peggy Coyne, Jeff Dietrich, Loui Lord Nelson, and George van Horn. It was through the Gates grant that I met my fabulous coauthor, friend, and UDL expert-extraordinaire Liz Berquist. She had a profound impact on the direction of the grant. We have continued to work together to guide fellow UDL travelers since then.

From Liz Berquist: My UDL journey started when I was a fairly new teacher in Baltimore County, Maryland. While attending a meeting with early UDL adopter Marsye Kaplan, I mentioned I was frustrated at the thought of adding flexible options to lessons after I had already planned my instruction. Marsye introduced me to UDL, and from there, I began to explore the framework as both a lesson design tool and a philosophy for including *all* learners. As I transitioned to Towson University as a doctoral student and faculty member, David Wizer, a passionate UDL advocate, introduced me to a community of like-minded individuals who were working toward including UDL in Maryland legislation (which eventually became part of our state code). While at Towson, I taught courses on UDL to many future educators and studied UDL and conceptual change as I completed my doctoral work with guidance from Bill Sadera. During this time, I was fortunate enough to become a member of the very first CAST faculty and had the privilege of learning from David Rose, Grace Meo, Peggy Coyne, Yvonne Domings, and the dedicated and passionate staff at CAST. An essential guidepost in my journey came from lessons learned during one of the first focused implementation projects, sponsored by CAST and the Bill and Melinda Gates Foundation and conducted in Baltimore County and Cecil County, Maryland; Chelmsford, Massachusetts; and Columbus, Indiana. During this work, I met the brilliant first author of this book, Patti Kelly Ralabate, who has become both a friend and professional mentor. This early implementation work connected early adopters of UDL from across the US; many of these individuals continue to blaze a UDL trail for others to travel, and I am grateful that they have become part of my UDL family:

George van Horn, Loui Lord Nelson, Nikki Norris, Billy Burke, Katie Novak, Lisa Carey, Joni Degner, Bryan Dean, and Jon Mundorf.

As you have learned, or will learn, UDL implementation requires careful reflection. I am consistently able to reflect on pieces of the UDL framework on a daily basis with many amazing educators, but I am especially grateful to Sean McComb, Jill Snell, Jeff Tessier, and Ben Berquist, who are the boots on the ground in our schools and who continually strive to find new ways to engage all learners. I'm also thankful that Juan Gallardo, Kirsten Omelan, Courtney Bensch, Rene Sanchez, and the teachers at Chavez High School in Houston, Texas, have been willing to engage in a five-year UDL journey and remain committed to finding new ways to implement the framework in a large, urban high school. Most recently, my view of the UDL framework has been challenged—as I seek to articulate how it can be used to ground practice in equitable access for those students who are most marginalized. For this new path in my journey, I owe a debt of gratitude to Lisa Williams, Tracey Durant, Heather Lageman, Jennifer Audlin, and Candace Logan-Washington. This UDL journey is not one to embark upon alone, and I am enriched by those who have traveled with me.

THIS BOOK IS FOR YOU

Your UDL journey may be just beginning or you may be well along your path. This book—*Your UDL Journey: A Systems Approach to Transforming Instruction*—is designed to offer guideposts along your way. It is an outgrowth of our continuous learning and joint experiences. We've poured our knowledge, skills, and passions into its pages in the hope of helping make your UDL journey successful.

A journey of a thousand miles must begin with a single step.

—LAO TZU, ancient Chinese philosopher

INTRODUCTION

OVERVIEW AND PURPOSE

The purpose of this book is to offer a guide—not a rigid step-by-step manual—for your UDL journey that is focused on adopting UDL as the conceptual framework for an entire system. Throughout the following chapters, the term *system* is used to refer to an environment that is larger than a single classroom—that is, a department, school, district, university, region, province, state, or country.

With this point in mind, the first three chapters (Section I) explain key concepts about systems change that impact your entire UDL journey. Section I defines UDL, implementation using a UDL approach, and relevant aspects of systems change. These overarching ideas will help you lay the foundation for achieving true transformation in how teachers plan their instruction and how learners experience the learning environment. For instance, rooting your UDL implementation in the identity and core values of those who work in your system will stabilize and fortify your efforts against interference and barriers you encounter along the way, and it will lead to sustainable transformation within your system.

In Section II, Chapters 4 through 8 describe pathways associated with each of the five UDL implementation phases. Each pathway is based on authentic experience—as well as implementation science, neuroscience, and systems change research—and designed as a goal or target to help you to channel your efforts during your UDL journey. The UDL framework is purposefully infused throughout your journey. For example, each implementation phase contains three pathways, each one aligned with one of the UDL principles: Engagement, Recognition, or Action and Expression. Also, the "Watch for UDL" boxes highlight specific instances where we prominently call out alignment of actions you might take with the UDL framework.

> **JOURNEY ALERT** As each phase is described, the Engagement pathway is presented first because of its crucial importance to sustainable change. No implementation model or leadership strategy can be successful if people are not interested in what you are doing or do not care to engage in the work.

Since UDL implementation is a process of continuous improvement, it's critical to continually ask, *"How will we know we have achieved our goal, objective, or target?"* To this end, suggestions for measuring your implementation efforts are consistently presented throughout pathway descriptions. Suggestions of ways to evaluate your progress as you pursue your UDL journey are described in the "Make It Actionable" sections.

Finally, Chapter 9 offers a call-to-action to the field with ideas for how you can go beyond UDL implementation.

Chapter Tools and Structure

Included in each chapter are two sets of questions that can be useful to you as an individual and to your team as you turn theory into actionable practice. Each chapter begins with "Guiding Questions" aimed at the big ideas addressed in that chapter. At the end of each chapter are "Essential Questions" to help you reflect on and apply key ideas. Essential Questions will be of particular interest to leadership and professional learning teams. Sprinkled throughout the book are tools referred to as "Spotlights," that propose opportunities to immediately apply suggestions, and "Whistle-Stops," which suggest resources that will help you extend your learning. Each chapter also includes specific immediate action steps under the heading "What Do We Do Now?" In alignment with the flexibility of UDL, not all recommendations need to be addressed. Feel free to choose those actions that are most applicable to your system and your journey.

At the end of the book is a "Resources" section that includes some longer tools such as surveys. You are free to copy and utilize these resources, but please be sure to include the following statement on any pages: "© 2020 CAST, Inc. Reprinted with permission. All rights reserved."

Now that we've discussed how this book provides you with the background knowledge, tools, and resources you will need for your UDL journey, let's get to it!

SECTION I

Transforming Instruction

Illustration by Eli Brophy, Philadelphia, PA

1

Why Is UDL a Transformative Framework?

GUIDING QUESTIONS

- Why is Universal Design for Learning (UDL) considered transformative?

- What's the difference between changing my instruction and transforming my school or district?

LET'S HEAR FROM NICOLE, A MIDDLE SCHOOL PRINCIPAL IN MARYLAND.

Once you learn about the UDL framework, you can't unsee it. I can recognize the guidelines in anything from an instructional practice to a school-wide or system initiative. We often talk about UDL as an umbrella. I really do believe that it encapsulates so many of the strategies that we are encouraged to incorporate in our practice, and I have not seen that in any other framework after almost twenty years in the field (Norris, personal interview, February 2018).

Nicole was in search of a framework to support school improvement. She recognized the variability that existed among her students, and she was adamant that any structure put in place honor and celebrate this diversity. She knew that teachers needed to provide accessible instruction that was engaging and supported students in becoming stronger learners. After learning about UDL at a workshop, she established professional learning teams and created a team of volunteers to guide her middle school staff through a process of adopting UDL as the school's instructional framework. Her beliefs about the power of the UDL implementation process are clear and unwavering.

> *The guidelines can be used in the design of professional development, as a frame for incorporating flexible strategies into the classroom and as a lens for discussion around relevant topics, like cultural responsiveness and equity-based inclusive practice. This is why UDL does not present a burden for teachers. Once they take the time to learn the framework, they are able to connect everything that they do with the UDL framework. UDL has helped our faculty to develop a common language of instructional expectations and instructional practices. This common language is essential in transforming instruction because it clarifies exactly what we are looking for in classrooms.*

Yet, Nicole readily admits that this change is not easy. She explains: "We've learned that instructional transformation is a process; it takes time."

For decades, educators like Nicole have sought ways to address persistent challenges of educational access, equity, and achievement. It's meant a constant process of change. And as Nicole realized, change is not easy. Sometimes barriers to change can appear insurmountable.

UDL and the Process of Change

Various change initiatives have been offered and tried in schools and districts across the US; however, one innovative framework has recently gained notoriety, influence, and respect in the field: Universal Design for Learning (UDL). As a matter of fact, UDL has been called ". . . one of the few big and truly transformative ideas to emerge in education over the past two decades" (Minow, 2009, p. ix). Read on to uncover how this chapter explores answers to these questions:

- What is UDL?
- What do we mean by UDL implementation?
- What is the difference between change and transformation?
- Why is UDL called a transformative framework?

> **REFLECTION** Perhaps you've been involved in a large-scale change initiative. What made it successful? What got in the way?

WHY UDL?

Let's start by clarifying what UDL is. *Universal Design for Learning (UDL)*, a conceptual framework based on cognitive neuroscience and learning science research, emerged nearly 25 years ago as an innovative approach to curriculum design and classroom instruction (Berquist, 2017). Originally defined by CAST, a nonprofit education research and design organization, UDL was introduced as a way to improve and optimize learning for students with disabilities.

Over the decades UDL has evolved. It is now recognized in federal education policy as a key approach for improving literacy instruction for all students (CAST, 2016). In the United States, Congress highlighted the potential impact of the UDL framework by including the following definition in the Higher Education Opportunity Act of 2008:

> *Universal Design for Learning (UDL) means a scientifically valid framework for guiding educational practice that—(A) provides flexibility in the ways information is presented, in the ways students respond or demonstrate knowledge and skills, and in the ways students are engaged; and (B) reduces barriers in instruction, provides appropriate accommodations, supports, and challenges, and maintains high achievement expectations for all students, including students with disabilities and students who are limited English proficient (CAST, 2016).*

When Congress reauthorized the Elementary and Secondary Education Act (ESEA) as the Every Student Succeeds Act (ESSA) in 2015, they again acknowledged UDL's potential and encouraged states to apply it to innovative assessment design, comprehensive literacy instruction, and ". . . personalized, rigorous experiences supported by technology" (CAST, 2016). Today, the UDL framework is applied to instruction in schools and universities all over the world (Rao, Currie-Rubin, & Logli, 2016). For educators like Nicole, UDL not only offers a way to create flexible learning environments, but it also provides a powerful tool for transforming how their systems advance the promise of effective instruction for *every* learner.

Later in this chapter, as we discuss UDL implementation, keep in mind that UDL is not a set of strategies or a method for individualizing services for students. Instead, it is an overarching approach or lens for viewing instructional and learning environment design. According to Meyer, Rose, and Gordon (2014), the UDL framework offers a set of three principles that require educators to provide

- multiple and flexible means of engagement to tap into diverse learners' interests, challenge them appropriately, and create motivation to learn;

- multiple and flexible means of representation of instructional content to offer students various ways of acquiring information and building knowledge; and

- multiple and flexible means of action and expression to provide diverse students with varied ways to plan and organize their learning and demonstrate what they have learned.

UDL and the Brain Networks

Each of the UDL principles is aligned with a set of networks in the brain that are used during learning:

- The *Principle of Engagement* corresponds to the affective networks that originate in the midbrain area and involve attention, motivation, and the learner's emotional response to what they perceive. These networks help learners to respond based on how they feel about the learning environment (the *why* of learning).

- The *Principle of Representation* corresponds to the recognition networks, originating from the back of the brain, which perceive information and assign meaning to it. They sense stimuli in the learning environment, guide information processing, identify patterns, and generalize knowledge across varying contexts (the *what* of learning).

- The *Principle of Action and Expression* corresponds to the strategic networks, originating in the front of the brain, which initiate and control purposeful actions and expression. They also include neural networks related to strategic planning, called *executive function skills*, that learners use to set goals and organize, sequence, and monitor their responses in the learning environment (the *how* of learning).

> **WHISTLE-STOP** If you'd like to learn more about UDL, see *Universal Design for Learning: Theory and Practice* (Meyer et al., 2014). To learn more about instructional design using UDL, see *Design and Deliver: Planning and Teaching Using Universal Design for Learning* (Nelson, 2016) and *Your UDL Lesson Planner: The Step-by-Step Guide for Teaching All Learners* (Ralabate, 2016).

In addition to individual teachers applying UDL to their lessons and learning environment design, groups of educators are adopting UDL as the conceptual framework for their entire systems, which may be defined as schools, districts, universities, regions, states, or provinces. When groups of educators engage in UDL implementation, it can affect entire systems.

Just one example is the transformation that has occurred within the Bartholomew Consolidated School Corporation (BCSC), a public-school system in Columbus, Indiana. Over a decade ago, BCSC adopted the UDL framework as the basis for its approach to curriculum and instruction for all learners. All BCSC educators are expected to apply UDL to their instructional planning. How has it made a difference? Since BCSC adopted the UDL framework, they have experienced significant changes in key data points—for instance, fewer students are being referred for special education services, performance of students who previously struggled on standardized assessments is improving (i.e., students with disabilities, students who received free and reduced lunch, and English learners), rates of participation in AP courses and AP exams have increased, and college readiness, demonstrated in ACT scores, has been enhanced (Quick, 2012; van Horn, 2015). BCSC continues to be a leading proponent of systemwide UDL implementation because they have seen the results.

Let's now turn to what systemic UDL implementation is and how it differs from a teacher's change in practice.

WHAT DO WE MEAN BY UDL IMPLEMENTATION?

First, let's be clear about what we mean by *implementation*. Implementation science researchers define implementation as "coordinated change at system, organization, program, and practice levels" (Fixsen, Naoom, Blase, Friedman, & Wallace, 2005, p. vi).

An individual teacher who makes intentional changes in her instructional practice by adopting the UDL framework is engaged in UDL implementation at a classroom or practice level. Groups of educators who decide to apply the UDL framework across classrooms, programs, schools, or sites are making systemic changes. Their work is at both the classroom level and large-scale system level (i.e., school, district, university, region, province, or state). Individual teachers can use a number of resources to guide their application of UDL to their individual instruction, but few explore UDL implementation as a large-scale change effort. This book focuses on systemic UDL implementation as a transformative process of continuous improvement.

The National Center on Universal Design for Learning defines UDL implementation in this way: "UDL implementation is not a set of discrete steps or protocols that everybody does in exactly the same way. It's a process: an iterative, continuously improving cycle of learning, reflection, and growth" (2012, p.1). It's important to underscore the aspect of customization implied by this definition. The UDL framework emphasizes flexibility and choice, as does the UDL implementation process. For a more detailed description of the UDL implementation process, see Chapter 3.

Common Elements Emerge

You may be familiar with scores of teachers who are applying UDL to their individual instruction, but you may not be aware of any schools or districts that are implementing UDL at a system level. Actually, numerous multiyear large-scale UDL implementation projects are underway across the United States and Canada and around the globe in locales such as Asia, Australia, Europe, the Middle East, and New Zealand (Berquist, 2017; New Zealand Ministry of Education, 2017; Nicol, 2014; Rao et al., 2016; Rappolt-Schlichtmann, Daley, & Rose, 2012). Respecting the concept of variability associated with UDL, each implementation project is unique.

UDL implementation projects differ in many ways. The sites range in academic levels from universities to preschool, elementary, middle, or high schools; and they differ in scope from individual schools to entire districts, regions, provinces, states, or countries (Berquist, 2017; Rappolt-Schlichtmann, Daley, & Rose, 2012). Many were initiated by teacher leaders, some by school or district administrators, and a few by state, provincial, regional, or national leaders. Early implementers were frequently assistive technology specialists or special educators, but today, more often than not, general education classroom educators and administrators are launching UDL implementation projects.

Although each site approaches implementation differently, we've observed seven common elements across sites related to participants' perspectives, values, and beliefs:

1. Shared dissatisfaction with the current situation
2. Shared recognition of a need for fundamental change
3. Shared belief that changing instruction or practice will make a difference
4. Shared desire to build inclusive environments
5. Shared understanding that systemic change takes time
6. Shared meaningful professional learning experiences
7. Consistent administrative support and engagement

Chapter 2 explores these common elements in more detail; however, the first two elements (i.e., dissatisfaction with the current situation and the need for fundamental change) require further explanation in the context of defining systemic UDL implementation.

WHAT IS THE DIFFERENCE BETWEEN CHANGE AND TRANSFORMATION?

CAST (2012) identifies a need for change as the beginning point for systemic UDL implementation. What do we mean by change? Within the context of schools, change has been defined as "... a process through which people and organizations move as they gradually come to understand, and become skilled and competent in the use of new ways" (Hall and Hord, 2001, pp. 4–5). Other definitions refine this one. For example, a famous psychologist who researched change and group dynamics, Kurt Lewin (1958), described change as complex, particularly within social organizations (e.g., schools). He believed that change was a learning process that was frequently unpredictable (Burnes, 2004; Kippenberger, 1998; Lewin, 1958). Key to his perspective is that learning is at the root of any change process.

Most UDL implementation projects focus on changing teachers' practice. Obviously, a change in practice requires teachers to learn how to do something differently. Chris McGoff, a business leader and organizational change consultant, states that change begins with the intent to alter the past to create an "improved version" that is "better, faster, cheaper, or some other 'er' word" (2012, p. 13). Interestingly, the stated goal of educators who adopt UDL as their instructional framework usually includes the words *better* or *improved*. For instance, they often note they want to *change* their instruction to *better* meet their learners' needs.

> **REFLECTION** What's your reason for learning more about UDL implementation? How does the definition of *change* resonate with you?

Dissatisfaction and a Need for Change

Why would you change your instruction? As Nicole suggested at the beginning of this chapter, change can be hard. And, change can be threatening. Human beings actually crave continuity and consistency (Deutschman, 2007). One obvious reason for adopting a new way of doing things is that you are dissatisfied with what you're doing now. The desire to adopt a new instructional framework such as UDL actually surfaces when educators begin to view their current practice as less effective or successful than it could be. This might seem obvious to you, but it's an important precondition to successful UDL implementation.

Dieting offers a good example: people who are happy with their weight or health don't choose to go on diets. You have to recognize that your weight is unreasonable or unhealthy before you're willing to make necessary changes in your diet. Likewise, teachers or administrators who are content with the results of their efforts are not interested in or willing to make modifications in their practice. Those who are dissatisfied are more likely to engage in substantive change. Educators who perceive a need to change and commit to making identified changes are, in fact, apt to achieve long-term successful results (Fixsen et al., 2005; Reeves, 2009; Senge et al., 1999).

> *Unless a community recognizes or accepts the premise that a change . . . is needed, . . . an innovative project has little hope of surviving, much less succeeding."*
>
> —PETERSILIA (CITED IN FIXSEN ET AL., 2005, p. 8)

According to Sadera and Hargrave (2005), dissatisfaction with the current situation is genuinely needed before change will occur, and it starts with teachers examining their beliefs. The authors identify three stages that occur as individuals alter their beliefs: pre-dissatisfaction, dissatisfaction, and post-dissatisfaction. It is during the dissatisfaction stage that new perceptions are compared with existing beliefs and, based upon the comparison, teachers determine a change is needed. Educators who are frustrated or unhappy with student achievement, engagement, or aspects of inclusivity may come to the conclusion that implementing UDL will result in better outcomes and willingly make a commitment to engage in the change process.

Change vs. Transformation

Before you begin your UDL journey, it's important to recognize that there is a substantial difference between *change* and *transformation.* Many educators who want to implement UDL seek an impact that goes beyond their classroom. In fact, they not only want to change their own instruction; they want to impact others' instructional design too. They desire a transformation in practice that will impact all learners. They are interested in changing their department, school, district, university, region, province, or state—that is, the whole system.

> *A butterfly is a transformation, not a better caterpillar.*
>
> —CHRIS MCGOFF, business consultant

As McGoff notes, "Change fixes the past. Transformation creates the future" (2012, p. 13). This definition points to the reality that there is a substantive difference between changing one's own practice (i.e., fixing what you already know and do) and seeking a transformation in instruction (i.e., creating a different future) across classrooms, departments, schools, or districts. Large-scale change or transformation is a long-term, sustainable process that goes beyond short-term fixes. True transformation impacts the system. Rather than just tinkering with old practices, transformation causes new structures and processes to emerge. It is only limited by your own creativity and persistence.

WHY IS UDL CALLED A TRANSFORMATIVE FRAMEWORK?

As individual teachers learn how to apply the UDL framework to their instruction, they begin to view learning and the learning environment differently. They focus on creating expert learners rather than covering curriculum (Meyer et al., 2014). Applied at the system level, the UDL implementation process affects more than a single classroom; its large-scale transformation happens at a system level and impacts groups of educators. The UDL implementation process can be called transformative because

- It applies implementation science and the UDL principles to guide educators in changing instruction across multiple learning environments.

- Its goal is large-scale systemic change in practice.

- Its intent is to offer educators the opportunity to create a long-term, sustainable process over time that results in continuous improvement in learner outcomes.

- Its purpose is to improve how each classroom supports learning as well as to change how teachers across classrooms, departments, schools, or districts meet all learners' needs.

Like the caterpillar who becomes a butterfly, the UDL implementation process aims to fundamentally transform how groups of educators view their instruction and their learners.

The UDL Flywheel Effect

Many initiatives have died or faded when teachers realized the change was just one more passing idea. In *All Systems Go,* Fullan (2010) makes the point that change can't be viewed as a "fad." Teachers won't commit the time and energy if they believe it will simply go away in the near future. They will hold back and take a wait-and-see posture rather than jump on board. In order for their intrigue to be heightened, they need to feel that adopting a new UDL lens for their instruction will help them make a significant difference *and* that it will endure. Once teachers sense its potential impact, UDL can catch fire!

If you've attended conferences or workshops focused on UDL implementation, you may have encountered a sense of collective excitement, almost euphoria, among groups of teachers who have decided to implement UDL across their learning environments. It is a sense of synergy—that together they can do more than they might do by themselves. Maybe you're feeling it right now.

In his seminal book on systems change, Collins (2001) describes what he calls the *flywheel effect*—the way that *good-to-great companies* affect change by sensing a buildup of momentum and aligning with it. Flywheels store energy over time and then release it quickly. They cause machines to experience energy rates that are typically beyond their original power. School teams who are beginning their UDL journey often feel this sense of collective power.

The importance of sensing that a collective movement is afoot is also alluded to by Fullan; he states "It is not alignment that makes all systems go but rather engagement and the power of allegiances put to a higher purpose" (Fullan, 2010, p. 37). Right now, you may be sensing the excitement and trepidation that comes with the UDL *flywheel effect*—a growing momentum among forward-thinking educators toward adopting UDL as a system-wide transformational framework. It emanates from a synergetic belief and expectation that implementing UDL in a systemic way will make a positive difference for all learners. If you're feeling it, spread it. The UDL flywheel effect can give you the stamina you need to power through the obstacles you may encounter on your UDL journey.

> *Efforts and courage are not enough without purpose and direction.*
>
> —JOHN F. KENNEDY, U.S. President

WHAT DO WE DO NOW?

Gather potential leadership team members. The group does not need to be more than four or five people, but make sure you have individuals who represent a spectrum of roles such as current decision makers, instructional leaders, and classroom educators. Depending on the envisioned breadth of your project, you may also want to include community, parental, and/or student representatives. If the team is so large that conversations are unwieldy, break into smaller cross-role discussion groups (e.g., three to four people).

Discuss how each educator views his current teaching situation. Use the Essential Questions that follow and/or the "Spotlight 1.1: Dissatisfaction and Willingness to Change" exercise.

SPOTLIGHT 1.1:
Dissatisfaction and Willingness to Change

Review the following statements. Which matches how you feel about your instruction? Ask your team or committee to reflect on and discuss these statements. Compare your responses and how they are or are not aligned.

I **don't see barriers** and am **unwilling** to make changes at this time.	I **see barriers** and am **willing** to make changes in my . . .
I **do see barriers** but am **unwilling** to make changes at this time.	I **see barriers,** am **willing** to make changes in my own practice, and **believe we can transform** our . . .

ESSENTIAL QUESTIONS

1. How do you view your current practice? What stage of satisfaction/dissatisfaction would apply to your perception of your teaching?

2. Are you satisfied with your outcomes? Or, are you experiencing barriers that prevent your learners from being successful?

3. To what extent is there a clear need to change?

4. How prepared are you to make changes in your own instructional approach?

5. Are you interested in and willing to work on changes that will transform instruction across classrooms, departments, schools, or districts?

6. In what ways could implementing UDL make a difference across classrooms or schools (i.e., the larger system)?

7. Have you been involved in large-scale or system-wide change initiatives before? How successful were they? To what extent did they result in a sustainable transformation in practice?

WHAT'S NEXT? Chapter 2 continues the discussion on UDL implementation at a system level by suggesting two key questions to ask as you start your UDL journey.

2

How Do We Get Started?

GUIDING QUESTIONS

- What are our first steps toward successful UDL implementation?
- How do we make sure what we do lasts?

LET'S HEAR FROM THE YSLETA INDEPENDENT SCHOOL DISTRICT IN TEXAS.

In some ways, the Ysleta Independent School District (YISD) is a typical public school district in Texas. Over 90% of the students are identified as having Hispanic backgrounds and more than one-third of the school population are English learners. Notably, YISD is committed to inclusive practices to support all learners. They have been for a long time. In fact, district leaders have dedicated almost a decade to focused professional learning designed to support students with disabilities in inclusive settings. Their work has included offering workshops on assistive technology and differentiated instruction, establishing an ongoing relationship with a professional development firm centered on building best practices in coteaching, and creating structures and supports to encourage general and special educators to design and deliver instruction together. After years of innovation, even with this laser-focus, special and general education were still viewed as separate entities and the district's work was seen as an inclusion initiative.

> *We fought so hard to make inclusion a reality, but once we had everyone together [general and special educators] we realized that something was still missing, and we asked ourselves "Now what do we do?" At that point, many of our team members had worked with the products that CAST had developed and read some of their articles on UDL. We had the perception that UDL was like differentiated instruction on steroids and we were beginning to apply the principles of UDL to our work in assistive technology. We knew what we wanted to do and where we wanted to go, but we couldn't quite name it or move it out of the "special ed" box (YISD team interview, March 2018).*

Elementary instructional planning teams included both special educators and general educators, which was a huge success for the district. And special education department leaders continued to collaborate with their colleagues in academics, ensuring that structures were in place to support co-planning partnerships at the elementary level. However, this effort did not quite bring about the transformation the team was seeking.

> *We had succeeded in bringing everyone to the table, but there was still a silo belief of "you work with these kids and I work with those kids." We physically had people in the same room but they had not truly made the philosophical shift we wanted. We explained our premise that what worked for learners with special needs was often beneficial for all, but we just did not have the foundational framework to rest this belief upon.*

It was at this point that the team realized they had reached a plateau in their journey toward their goal of creating a true conceptual shift. They began reaching out to teachers and visiting classrooms, looking for patterns that would inform their work. They heard over and over again that teachers did not believe they were meeting the diverse needs of their students. They needed assistance. Although teachers did not use the term *learner variability*, leadership recognized it as the underlying concern and realized that it was a perfect time to introduce the UDL framework.

> *The whole variability thing is what brought it home for us as a team. We had the groundwork already laid and we realized that the UDL framework would help our teachers to see how their work was connected. It became the lens that covered*

everything that was already in place, but also filled in the gaps and gave us the language to put our vision into actionable practices.

District leaders decided to recruit four campuses for an initial UDL implementation project designed to blend professional development workshops with job embedded professional learning communities. Because they had already been collaboratively planning for three years, school teams were able to make a quick start. Learning about UDL as a lens to address learner variability was a natural fit. As teachers learned about UDL, they revisited their current beliefs and practices and real change started to happen. They now see implementing UDL as causing the conceptual change they envisioned.

The UDL framework helped us to move beyond the WHAT of supporting all learners and into the WHY and the HOW. One of the most beneficial aspects has been the common language we developed; UDL has helped us have better conversations and more focused planning meetings. We have moved to discussing what all students need rather than concentrating only on our students with special needs. The language of multiple options for all has permeated all of our instructional conversations.

A Need for Change

You'll recall that Chapter 1 highlighted the importance of recognizing *a need for change* as the starting point for UDL implementation efforts. The Ysleta Independent School District staff certainly did just that. Their journey started when they realized that separate learning environments weren't working for all their learners, particularly those with special needs. They needed to make a change. Notice how their approach centered on their core values, beliefs, and priorities:

- They valued inclusiveness.

- They believed they needed to end the disparate views of teachers toward students with and without disabilities.

- They began their UDL implementation journey with a clear priority—to support all learners in inclusive learning environments.

The following are ideas that will help you do the same thing.

START WITH WHO AND WHY

Once you become familiar with the UDL framework and recognize the need for change, you may be tempted to launch into your implementation objective or what you want to accomplish. Setting goals is certainly a crucial aspect of the UDL implementation process; however, first take a moment for reflection and discovery. Since the transformation quest is fraught with unanticipated barriers, unavoidable mistakes, and unforeseen complications, you need to begin your UDL journey with a strength-based foundation that provides a clear picture of

- who you are as a team,
- what your educators value,
- what your educators believe about their instruction,
- what your educators are willing to change, and
- why your educators are interested in making a change.

Rather than immediately starting with *what* you want to do, take the time to ask two critical questions: *Who?* and *Why?*

Question #1: Who Are We?

Gathering your team to discuss data regarding your students, employees, and community will help you clarify what Senge and associates call your *current reality* (Senge et al., 1999). Essentially, this information reveals your system's identity or self-image.

> **REFLECTION** How well do you think your system's self-image aligns with your personal self-image?

Why spend time on this? Your current reality is the basis for your shared vision or desired future. Other benefits of engaging in this group self-reflection include

- While your team jointly contemplates who you are, they build a common understanding of your strengths, needs, purpose, priorities, and the core values and beliefs that will guide your decision-making (Kim & Corey, 2008).

- This group-think process creates the capacity of leaders and teachers to think, envision what could be, and collaboratively solve problems together.

- You gain insights into how much investment and support may be expected from inside and outside your system and what type or amount of change may be tolerable.

See "Spotlight 2.1: Who Are We?" at the end of this chapter for examples of questions to explore.

After you analyze your system's descriptive data, refine your system's self-image or current reality by examining its core values and beliefs about learning. *Beliefs* are basic assumptions we make about the world; *core values* stem from our beliefs. No matter how large or small, these ideas make your system what it is. According to the New England Association of Schools and Colleges (NEASC) (2016), core values and beliefs about learning are qualities that are foundational to the system's learning expectations. They shape the culture and set the priorities within the system. For instance, educators in YISD valued collaboration and meeting the diverse needs of their learners. Although educators identify hundreds of qualities as core values, they typically include collaboration, respect, personal integrity, equity, intellectual curiosity, and appreciation of diversity (NEASC, 2016). In many cases, your school or district has established core values and a mission statement. These are good resources to use to launch your investigation.

The experience of successful implementation changes practice as well as attitudes and beliefs about instruction (Guskey, 2002). Research shows that educators tend to try new ideas out by assessing them based on whether they fit within their own values and beliefs about teaching and learning (Richardson, 1998). If they fit, they're adopted. If they don't fit, they're discarded. Established over an entire lifetime, educators' core values and beliefs are not easily influenced (Hunzicker, 2004). Why is this important to know? Since a change in practice is integral to teachers willingly altering beliefs about their instruction, the initial focal point of your UDL implementation project needs to go beyond the system's stated core values and beliefs. You need to zero in on teachers' personal beliefs about their teaching and your project's focus needs to be on changing teachers' *beliefs* as well as their actions (Guskey, 2002; Hunzicker, 2004; Sadera & Hargrave, 2005).

The only person who is educated is the one who has learned how to learn and change.

—CARL ROGERS, American psychologist

Question #2: Why Are We Adopting UDL?

Knowing your system's identity or current reality clarifies strengths and needs and naturally leads to examining your rationale for adopting UDL. For example, if underachievement is a major element of your system's current reality, your reason for implementing UDL might be to increase access to rigorous instruction for all learners. Like YISD, if your system's identity includes segregated classrooms that do not hold students with special needs to high expectations, your motive could be to provide an inclusive learning environment that challenges all learners. Or, if the current reality for your system is that a high percentage of students are dropping out or are truant, your desire may be to offer an engaging, personalized curriculum for all students. Conducting a needs assessment at this point will ensure that your rationale is rooted in authentic data. There are as many purposes for adopting UDL as there are systems.

> **WHISTLE-STOP** If you'd like to know more about conducting a needs assessment and UDL implementation, see *Universally Designed Leadership: Applying UDL to Systems and Schools* (Novak & Rodriguez, 2016).

In addition to linking the rationale for your UDL implementation project with identified system needs, connect the project's intent with ideas that are personally relevant to teachers. Making this project personal aligns well with the UDL framework because it engages your team's affective networks. Consider asking each member of the team to identify personal rationales or outcomes that they want to achieve in addition to those that are also devised for the project. Later, if or when dips in enthusiasm occur or project participants feel pulled in different directions, they can reconnect to their personal rationales as well as the project's mutual purpose to help them address those distractions and challenges.

Fullan (2010) makes several points about why educators do what they do that are worth reviewing. He points out that most teachers join the profession because they want to make a difference in the lives of their students. In addition, although educators will agree that "all students can learn," some may not really believe it. They become believers when they actually achieve success with specific students who have been struggling.

> *In order to succeed, we must first believe that we can.*
>
> —NIKOS KAZANTZAKIS, Greek writer

To kick off a discussion on their personal relevancy, ask your team members these questions:

- Why do you do what you do as an educator?
- How does your response relate to our project's rationale?

Keeping these key observations in mind as your team members evaluate the personal relevance of the project will help them to avoid disillusion over time.

REFLECTION Reasons for joining a UDL implementation project differ. A few may want to enhance their personal image or position. Some are interested in increasing knowledge or skills. Others seek comradery. How does personal relevancy affect your engagement?

Question #3: What Does It Look Like?

Let's consider an example of how this approach might work. Before the Ysleta Independent School District initiated their UDL implementation project, they offered a variety of instructional enhancements that they thought would make a difference. But there was no difference. Once they identified inclusiveness as one of their core values, they aligned their UDL implementation project with their belief that inclusive learning environments better meet the needs of all learners. They established a new priority—teaching educators to use a UDL lens to view their instruction—and as a result, teachers made a needed conceptual shift. They started to think differently about their instruction and began to use UDL to focus on what all students needed instead of only on what students with disabilities needed.

Another example of what it looks like when you link your UDL implementation project with your system's values is the approach taken by Bartholomew Consolidated School Corporation (BCSC), a public school district in Columbus, Indiana. When they started their successful UDL journey in 2002, they highlighted the alignment between the district's core values and the UDL framework, particularly their expressed belief that "all students can learn" (Bartholomew Consolidated School Corporation, 2009, slide 2). To address the personal learning needs of each student, they agreed that their first priority was to bring together all the various district projects and initiatives under UDL as the overarching framework for their system. Every new initiative had to align with UDL and their core belief that "all students can learn." With this steadfast alignment between their core values and their UDL implementation process, BCSC continues to make sustainable, continuous improvement in instruction.

A Group Commitment

You may have already decided that implementing UDL at a system level is the answer. That's why you're reading this book, right? But to achieve sustainable transformation, this decision must be a group or team commitment. No matter how fabulous you are as a leader, you cannot do this alone. As the YISD team discovered, their desire to build inclusive learning environments remained unfulfilled even after years of effort. Their self-examination helped them to develop a *mutual belief* that changing instruction would make a difference. When they committed as a group to adopt UDL, they began to see a realization of their desired future—inclusive classrooms.

> *Never doubt that a small group of thoughtful, committed citizens can change the world; indeed, it's the only thing that ever has.*
>
> —MARGARET MEAD, cultural anthropologist

Chapter 4 shares strategies for defining your shared vision. Before you determine a vision or specific goal for your project, it's valuable to compare your current reality with a broad idea of your desired future. If these two images are already closely aligned, there may be no real momentum for changing anything. Rather than expending energy and funds on a project that may accomplish very little, you can arguably stop now.

However, it is more likely that you'll uncover significant unrealized core values and/or unmet priorities. They become the bedrock for change. And, because your UDL implementation project is rooted in your system's core identity, including your unrealized core values or unmet priorities, your project has a strong foundation.

UNDERSTANDING TRANSFORMATION AS SYSTEMS CHANGE

Whether you're considering an implementation project for your department, school, district, university, region, or state, you are part of a system that is larger than a single classroom. Your system is likely complex—perhaps even chaotic—and made up of a variety of components, including physical structures, processes, and people. What is common among all systems is that they pull together various elements to achieve a common purpose (Betts, 1992).

First applied to sociocultural systems in the 1930s and 1940s by Lewin, systems theory looks at the dynamics within systems. For decades, businesses and large organizations have used systems theory to achieve dramatic transformations in how they are organized and how they respond to the ebb and flow of cultural and societal shifts. A myriad of books and organizational change consultants are available to facilitate large-scale transformation.

> *Systems thinking is a discipline for seeing wholes. It is a framework for seeing interrelationships rather than things, for seeing "patterns of change" rather than static "snapshots."*
>
> —PETER SENGE, systems scientist

It's not necessary to study systems change theories in order to plan a successful UDL implementation project. But there are 10 lessons from systems change research that are especially beneficial to consider as you move forward:

1. Relationships are more important than outcomes.
2. Perceptions shape interactions and impact success.
3. Learning to listen, trust, and empower others trumps skill-building.
4. Gathering a cross-section of people together creates a powerful, invaluable resource.
5. Outcomes emerge through an iterative process of trial and error.
6. Systems transform their structures dramatically in response to feedback.
7. Transformation reverberates through the entire system in unpredictable ways.
8. Periods of instability can be expected as new ideas and practices are assimilated into the system.
9. Transformation appears to move in a back-and-forth motion or a spiral more than a straight line.
10. Systemic change takes time.

(Burnes, 2004; Fullan, 1999; Hall & Hord, 2001; Kippenberger, 1998; Lewin, 1958; Schalock & Fredericks, 1994; Senge et al., 1999; Stacey, 1996).

> **WHISTLE-STOP** If you'd like to learn more about systems-thinking or large-scale organizational change, look at the works by A. Hargreaves, Fullan, Kim, and Senge cited in our "References" section. Free online resources are also available from The Systems Thinker at *https://thesystemsthinker.com/sectors/education/*.

Your UDL implementation project may or may not orchestrate profound systemic change. The important aspect of applying systems change theories to your project planning is to recognize that you and your team members are all part of the larger system. There are things you can affect or control and those that you can't. Because you exist within the larger system, you can look for ways to leverage elements outside your project's environment, but you should also be on the lookout for factors outside your project that can negatively affect your success.

WHAT DO WE DO NOW?

Gather your leadership team. If your team doesn't currently include a cross-section of people who represent a variety of roles within your system, add those individuals. Your team will be more productive and successful if it consists of members who volunteer—they are there not because they have been coerced but because they are committed to working with the team to make a difference. Provide resources that will help your team to develop your system's identity. Use Spotlight 2.1 to define your system's identity and core values.

SPOTLIGHT 2.1:
Who Are We?

Step 1: Define Your Current Reality

Task A: Ask the group to synthesize information about your system into an agreed-upon, one-sentence description of your system. If the answers to any questions are unknown to you, use website resources or ask state, district, or school leaders for assistance. They are often very familiar with these types of data and rankings. Here are examples of questions to consider:

1. Do you serve a small, rural community, a medium-sized suburban area, or a large, urban one?
2. Are a large number of students migratory?
3. How diverse are the economic backgrounds of your students? For instance, are students primarily from low-income or middle-income neighborhoods, or is there a wider distribution?
4. How many students are the children or grandchildren of town council or school board members, professional white-collar workers, and shopkeepers who are long-standing, active pillars in the community?
5. How many students enter the military after graduation?
6. What percentage of students are recent immigrants?
7. What percentage of students are English learners?
8. What percentage of students have disabilities or special needs?
9. Compared with other schools or districts, is yours viewed as low-performing or high-performing?
10. Are you known as the place to escape from or the place to be?
11. How many teachers live in or are well-known in the community?
12. How many educators are graduates of your school or district?

13. How many educators have advanced degrees or are currently in school studying for advanced degrees?

14. Are teachers able to support their households on their salaries or do they typically need to have additional jobs?

15. What percentage of educators retire each year?

16. Are there trends in your data that point to a future identity that looks substantially different than the present (e.g., an increase in a population with specific needs, an improvement in graduation rates over time, an anticipated increase in teacher retirements requiring new staff hires, or dramatic decreases in funding)?

Step 2: Clarify Your Core Values

Task B: Identify individual attributes and agreed-upon, jointly held core values.

Ask team members to

1. Individually identify no more than three (3) core values that relate to their practice as an educator and leader and write them down. Explain that *values* are qualities that are considered worthwhile or desirable.

2. Share their core values with someone else on the team, preferably someone they know and trust. Don't debate them. Each person should determine their own values.

3. Discuss the sets of core values in groups of two or three to clarify their meaning and refine the list as values and *not* aspirations. Discuss how they may be alike or different from each other. Note items that support similar concepts. Combine duplicated concepts. Items that are not values should be reframed as values or eliminated.

4. Compile a refined list of all the core values identified by all team members.

5. As a group, compare the lists from the subgroups and organize the identified core values under categorical headings, matching like values. Again, note similarities and combine duplicated concepts. Narrow the list as much as possible aiming for no more than 10 core values. Do not discard values just because they are unique, outliers, or unlike others.

6. As individuals, rank the entire list in order of importance. Evaluate list items based on which values take precedence. Which will team members honor over another?

7. Combine the rankings into one ranked list. Reconcile outliers by asking the group whether the outliers could be combined with another item. In some cases, recognizing that the outlier is important but is not a mutually-agreed-upon value will spur the group to move it off the combined list.

Present the combined list as the foundational core values for your UDL implementation project.

ESSENTIAL QUESTIONS

1. How could UDL implementation build upon our current identity?
2. In what ways could implementing UDL address our weaknesses?
3. Who wants to be involved? Who needs to be involved?
4. To what extent is our team empowered to make decisions that may impact the system as a whole?
5. How can we leverage our common beliefs and core values to move forward?

WHAT'S NEXT? Chapter 3 applies implementation science to define and describe the five phases of the UDL implementation process.

3

What Is the UDL Implementation Process?

GUIDING QUESTIONS

- What makes the UDL implementation process different?
- How can UDL be a lens for transformation?

LET'S HEAR FROM THE ALGONQUIN AND LAKESHORE CATHOLIC SCHOOL DISTRICT BOARD, ONTARIO, CANADA.

For over 20 years, the Algonquin and Lakeshore Catholic School District Board, a public school system located in Ontario, Canada, has been consistently committed to supporting every student in their home school with a focus on full inclusion. In 2011, the system entered a visioning process and thoughtfully considered what inclusion should look like in all their schools. Their UDL journey is an example of how the UDL implementation process can be transformative:

> *We asked ourselves, what must children need to be successful? This visioning led us to reconsider how our spaces could reflect flexibility and access to information. We*

recognized that spaces in our schools enabled a context for learning and collaboration and we understood that learners could achieve more if we designed to support variability in advance. We started by transitioning our libraries to learning commons. At the same time that we were working to redesign our physical spaces, we also canvassed the district, meeting with the staff of every school and every administrator in order to hear firsthand how the district commitment to inclusion was being put into actionable practice (ALCSD Board interview, May 2018).

This course of action allowed the district leadership to identify successful strategies and system initiatives and to uncover systematic barriers preventing schools from progressing toward more inclusive, learner-centered environments. District leadership clearly heard from a majority of staff members who agreed with the district vision of celebrating and valuing student strengths and designing a curriculum that is accessible to all learners. This commitment to full inclusion was embedded into the belief system of the district, but additional supports and structures to move these beliefs into practice were needed.

We realized that we can't be doing this work in different compartments. Although our goals in curriculum, learning technologies, and special education were parallel, we began to see that initiative fatigue was setting in, and our innovations would not take hold unless we took down the barriers and began to work together. This is when we started to consider UDL at the leadership level.

At that time, the core leadership team participated in the Harvard UDL Summer Institute and was introduced to UDL as an implementation process.

We began to really see UDL as the glue of our work; participation in the Harvard Institute gave us the opportunity to become like-minded across the central leadership support network. We began to look at our own barriers, build a core team, and design a plan for our system that put UDL and student-centered pedagogy at the heart of our work.

This process was a smooth transition since district leaders for the Algonquin and Lakeshore Catholic School District had previously begun exploring UDL as a framework for redesigning school learning spaces. Their laser-focus on accessibility and flexibility quickly made an impact in the transformation of shared spaces, positively impacting student engagement and providing a physical representation of the district's core beliefs. At the same time, leadership realized that the UDL framework could also be used as tool to guide district-level decision-making and move instructional transformation beyond just providing access. The district leadership committed to providing multiple options for professional learning related to UDL and began to consider their journey toward UDL implementation as a process itself. The UDL principles were embedded into all professional learning, first in leadership networks and then in teacher professional learning. To hasten their work, the district called on UDL leaders in the field and utilized the CAST implementation process as they embarked on their UDL journey.

REFLECTION How receptive to flexibility and choice is your system?

THE UDL IMPLEMENTATION PROCESS— AN OVERVIEW

In 2010, a grant from the Bill and Melinda Gates Foundation tasked CAST, a nonprofit research organization focused on UDL, with investigating, developing, and piloting a systems-change approach to professional learning and school improvement employing UDL as the overarching framework. During the project, CAST worked with educators from four US school districts, to craft the UDL implementation process. Each district was uniquely situated along a continuum of UDL implementation. They represented different profiles of strengths, needs, and familiarity with UDL and offered a variety of examples of implementation challenges and successes (Ganley & Ralabate, 2013).

UDL as a Lens

To develop the UDL implementation process, CAST braided neuroscience and implementation science research, applied the authentic experiences of educators, and intentionally infused the UDL framework. Consequently, the UDL implementation process is characterized by flexibility, choice, and a respect for the learner variability represented in every group, including your implementation team and your system's educators. As CAST states: "This is an important distinction that makes UDL implementation different from other initiatives that attempt to hold participants to a specific, regimented implementation approach" (National Center on Universal Design for Learning, 2012, p. 1).

The UDL implementation process offers a customizable series of professional learning and coaching options and flexible resources and tools (CAST, 2012). Its purpose is to serve as a decision-making guide for educators who are adopting the UDL framework at a large-scale systems level. It is not meant to be a formula or recipe. It is an outline of pathways along your UDL journey that offers you signposts and reflection points to keep you moving forward. It applies a UDL lens to large-scale change in practice.

FIVE PHASES OF UDL IMPLEMENTATION

Adapted from the National Implementation and Research Network's original implementation research, the five phases of the UDL implementation process are (1) Explore, (2) Prepare, (3) Integrate, (4) Scale, and (5) Optimize (CAST, 2012; Fixsen et al., 2005). These five phases describe how you can prepare for UDL implementation, address systematic integration of the UDL framework with other current initiatives and practices, scale effective policies, procedures and practices system-wide, and build sustainability.

Throughout this book, when we mention a system, we are referring to any complex learning environment—a group of classrooms, a school, university, district, region, state, province, or country. These environments are all systems. Since each system will proceed differently, the five phases are fluid and recursive in nature rather than rigid stages. The process will vary. For example, as you move forward, you may observe that your system tends to progress in a sequential fashion through the five phases, you may see an overlap between some phases, or you could repeat a specific phase in an iterative manner as your system strengthens and improves. This flexible process of progression accounts for the variability of your system's learners, including educators, who are also learners. It also offers multiple options for designing learning opportunities and environments that meet the learning needs of all learners within your system (Berquist, 2017).

WATCH FOR UDL

It's important to note that the five phases of the UDL implementation process are purposefully aligned with the UDL principles to include options for engagement, representation, and action and expression. Specifically, each phase includes three proposed pathways that address how to (1) *engage* team members and individuals within your system, (2) *represent* information to individuals within and outside your system to build knowledge and understanding, and (3) offer options for *action and expression* with a particular focus on strategic, proactive planning.

CAST created a graphic to display the iterative, cyclical aspects of the UDL implementation process (CAST, 2012); see Figure 3.1. Note that in the center of the spiral is a Need for Change and it continues through the five phases, finally ending in Expert Learning—the ultimate goal of UDL and the UDL implementation process. Listed on the right-hand side of the spiral are the UDL guidelines and the three UDL principles (i.e., representation, action and expression, and engagement), which interface throughout the process.

In this next section, each of the five phases of the UDL implementation process is briefly defined. Thorough phase descriptions can be found in subsequent chapters.

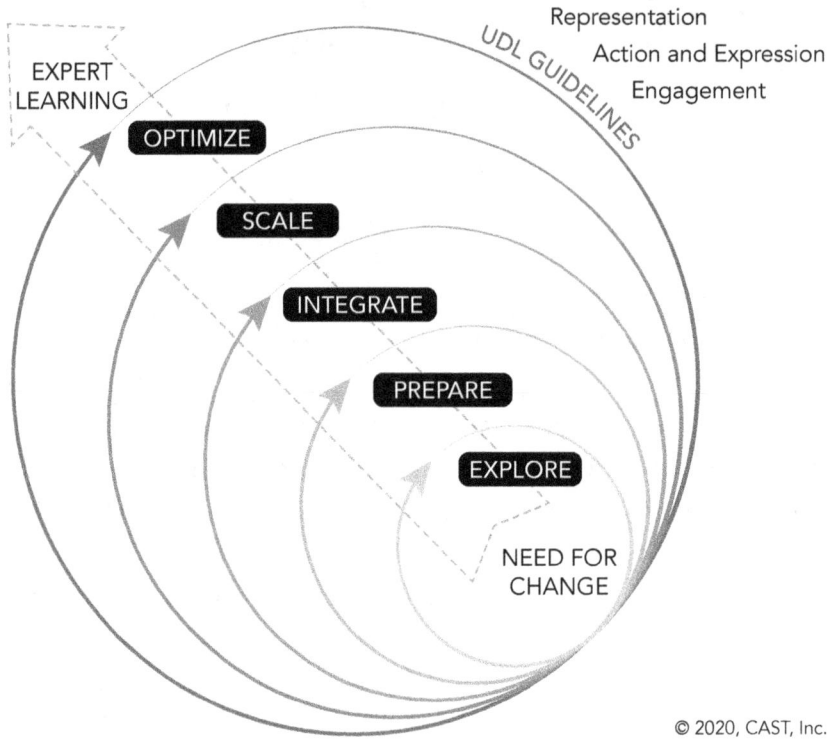

FIGURE 3.1: The UDL implementation process

Explore

During this phase, you will (1) *assess readiness* by determining interest and willingness to apply UDL as an implementation process, (2) *investigate UDL* as a potential framework for system-wide curriculum design and decision-making, and (3) *build awareness* about UDL among key decision makers within and outside of your system.

Prepare

During the Prepare phase, you will (1) *create a UDL climate* that respects variability and accepts it as the rule throughout your system, (2) conduct a self-reflection to *map resources* and determine which system policies, processes, structures, and practices might need to change, and (3) *define measurable outcomes* and an action plan.

Integrate

You will concentrate on providing professional learning opportunities during the Integrate phase with specific goals to (1) *foster collaboration* to hasten the infusion of UDL into learning environments; (2) *develop educator expertise* by providing customized professional learning opportunities, including UDL-focused professional development workshops, professional learning communities (PLCs) and coaching; and (3) *evaluate* the efficacy of established policies, processes, and procedures, infusing the UDL principles as needed, and *create* new practices that align with the UDL framework.

Scale

When you are ready to scale your UDL implementation project, you will engage in steps that acknowledge and extend UDL as a system-wide framework. You will (1) *promote a UDL community of practice* that supports shared collaborative system-wide learning; (2) *expand practices* to create an integrated, system-wide approach to instruction and decision-making; and (3) *enhance effective implementation* through policies, processes, procedures, and organizational structures infused with the UDL principles.

Optimize

During the Optimize phase, you will (1) *nurture a UDL culture* throughout your system, (2) *maximize improvement* by embedding practices and iterative processes that balance stability with innovation, and (3) strategically *predict, respond, and plan for* internal and external challenges that could impact UDL implementation. This phase focuses on continuous improvement and building the long-term sustainability of your UDL project.

PROACTIVE PLANNING OVERCOMES OBSTACLES

It's important to keep in mind the following aspect of UDL implementation: although most UDL leadership teams will follow the UDL implementation phases and pathways in a logical, linear manner, some won't. Based on the variability and uniqueness of your system, you can and will add innovation to the pathways and ideas presented in this book. That's expected.

The UDL implementation process offers a strategic guide to your UDL project. Nevertheless, no matter how organized or well-planned, you can expect to encounter challenges and barriers along your UDL journey that can affect your success. You will anticipate some of these impediments. A few will be complete surprises.

> *All successful schools experience "implementation dips" as they move forward.*
>
> —MICHAEL FULLAN, educational leadership expert

One way to thwart unexpected detours in your UDL journey is to proactively plan to address obstacles along the way. Drawing on the wisdom of various researchers and organizational change consultants, here are some suggestions to do exactly that.

Understand Who You Are

Clarifying your system's identity and core values will ensure relevancy and provide steady footing for your UDL journey. Your decision making will rest on your system's identify and your core values, thereby helping you steer clear of bird walks that take you away from your system's authenticity, purpose, and mission.

Define a Clear Shared Vision

Over the past 30 years, education researchers have identified several elements that characterize highly effective schools and successful instructional change efforts (Fullan, 1993; Marzano, 2003; Ragland, Clubine, Constable, & Smith 2002). Chief among them is a common or shared vision, which builds consensus and answers why you are working together. Your project's vision should emerge from your system's beliefs and identify need for change. Without a joint commitment to achieving your shared vision, educators can become distracted by other issues and pressures, and, as a result, transformational change will be unlikely. However, establishing a clear, shared vision for your UDL implementation project can buttress the impact of unexpected challenges along the way. For example, some project teams we've worked with voice a joint desire to build inclusive learning environments or they express their mutual belief that changing instruction or practice will improve their student outcomes. They hold fast to their desire to make a difference even when adversity tries to impede their progress.

Your shared vision should be a mutually desired future that is developed and agreed upon by your project team. It should be a collective goal that could not be achieved individually. Without a shared vision, a team is *not* actually a team, but rather a co-acting group (Hackman, 2002). All educators who join your effort should embrace this shared vision because this consensus will form the basis for your work, guide your decision-making, and provide an important standard with which to measure your success.

If you want to go quickly, go alone. If you want to go far, go together.

—AFRICAN PROVERB

Aim High

Don't be afraid to set ambitious, audacious goals. Aiming high will optimize motivation and performance. If this concept seems unrealistic to you or you'd prefer to start small by focusing on what's achievable in the immediate future, consider establishing intermediate steps or short-term objectives that build toward your more audacious future. Starting small doesn't prevent you from upholding inspiring ultimate outcomes. You can build excitement and a sense of accomplishment as you meet each of your short-term objectives. If we use a fitness analogy, working toward the ultimate goal of running a marathon might start with maintaining your running pace for 15 minutes, then increasing it to 30 minutes, and so on.

Setting high expectations for your UDL implementation project is based on an underlying premise of UDL, namely that all learners can become expert learners who are knowledgeable, resourceful, and strategic (Meyer, et al. 2014). Keep in mind that the goal of becoming expert learners applies to the adults within your system as well as the students. Although most, if not all, of your team members may already think of themselves as expert learners, each one can also aspire to become a *UDL expert* by engaging in your UDL implementation project.

Share Leadership

Hollywood movies romanticize the image of the lone education reformer who single-handedly and dramatically transforms a "troubled" school into a high performer. Yet, the reality is that long-term sustainability using this type of top-down leadership model is often short-lived or stymied when the leader leaves the system. Consistent administrative support and the participation of key decision makers is certainly critical to the success of your UDL journey. Nevertheless, practicing shared leadership is much more likely to lead to sustainable transformation (Hargreaves & Fink, 2009). It offers your project the collective wisdom of all your team members and builds staying power.

> *Alone, we can do so little. Together, we can do so much.*
>
> —HELEN KELLER, author and political activist

How do you know that you are employing shared leadership? Look for these six characteristics:

1. **Equity.** Distribution of leading and learning opportunities is transparent among all team members.
2. **Balance.** Role disbursement is balanced among team members who rotate facilitating discussions, presenting knowledge content, and creating resources.
3. **Consensus.** The unequivocal commitment to consensus leads to decisions based on mutual understanding and agreement.
4. **Trust.** Interdependent trust and respectful relationships develop because all team members' perspectives are valued.
5. **Growth.** The team's collective capacity is enhanced while individual skills are enriched.
6. **Synergy.** Team members sense their collective impact is greater than their individual actions.

The goal of shared leadership is authentic *engagement,* not just *participation* (Cashman et al., 2014). Certainly, a shared leadership approach aligns well with the UDL framework because a chief tenet of UDL is that all learners should be meaningfully engaged in their own learning. The same holds true for the adults on your team and in your system. It also stems from a "build our own" mindset because future leaders develop from within your team and are then able to step into decision-making roles when needed.

Embed Incentives

From the very beginning, consider resources your team will need to bolster and sustain their efforts. Think about why educators in your system will want to join the journey. Are there incentives that might spike initial interest, such as stipends, release time, credits toward recertification, special awards or recognition, additional instructional resources, or enhanced evaluation procedures?

Team engagement also means fostering collaboration by encouraging interactions and opportunities to exchange views. Be careful not to mistake mere participation for true involvement. Team members may attend meetings and professional learning activities but not be truly engaged. Yes, learning new strategies and being more successful with learners are motivating aspects. But, frankly, they may not be strong enough to sustain effort because consistent impediments present themselves during a multiyear project. To support persistence and sustain active, meaningful engagement, think about ways to address participants' affective networks. For example, highlight publicly the educators who make a commitment to the project, build positive relationships and a sense of belonging among team members, and insert fun into what you're doing. Recognize team members with awards, such as "UDL innovator." Get involved with the UDL Implementation and Research Network (*www.udl-irn.org*), an international volunteer group that supports communities of practice. Doing so might help your team members feel the synergy they need to persist through the ebb and flow of your UDL journey.

Assess Progress

Set intermediate objectives and build in periodic checks and assessments of your progress. Revisit your engagement strategies intermittently to be sure they are still effective. If you find that you've wandered away from your mission, you'll be able to quickly make course corrections. Another advantage to periodic assessments is that they give you opportunities to celebrate your successes. Make sure you celebrate! Highlighting milestones you've reached for the project as well as individual achievements promotes continued commitment. Suggestions for assessments and progress checks (i.e., check-ins) are highlighted throughout this book.

Provide Shared Meaningful Professional Learning Experiences

Ultimately, the success of your UDL project depends upon the collective knowledge, skills, and dispositions of your team members. Just like any group of learners, variability is to be expected. There are a variety of ways to increase team members' knowledge and skills and no one way works for every educator. Although effective professional learning strategies will be described in later chapters, it's important to keep in mind the following overarching concepts as you begin your UDL journey:

> **Relationships are paramount.** As Payne (1995) stated, "No significant learning occurs without a significant relationship" (p. 211–212). Successful professional learning is rooted in relationships that develop as educators engage in shared experiences.
>
> **Flexibility is key.** Professional learning is more effective when it is a personalized experience. Each team member needs the autonomy to choose learning options that work best for them.
>
> **Apply UDL to professional learning.** As Berquist (2017) reminds us, "The golden rule when presenting on UDL is to model it in your practice" (p. 5). UDL is best understood when it is experienced as a learner. Educators need to have the opportunity to apply the UDL conceptual framework to their current beliefs about learning and actively explore meaningful ways to apply it to their own instruction.
>
> **Keep it authentic.** The most effective professional learning occurs "as teachers plan lessons together, examine their students' work to find ways to improve it, observe one another teach, and plan improvements based on various data" (Killion, Roy, & von Frank, 2009, p. 27).

Table 3.1 applies two of the UDL principles (i.e., engagement and action and expression) in a crosswalk with implementation practices to illustrate how UDL serves as a lens for your implementation process.

TABLE 3.1: UDL Implementation Crosswalk

ENGAGEMENT	ACTION AND EXPRESSION
Self-regulation Promote expectations and beliefs that optimize motivation by aiming for high expectations.	**Executive functions** Guide appropriate goal-setting by defining a clear, shared vision.
Sustain effort and persistence Facilitate personal coping skills and strategies by embedding incentives.	**Executive functions** Support planning and strategy development by employing shared leadership.
Sustain effort and persistence Foster collaboration and community by providing meaningful, shared professional learning experiences.	**Executive functions** Enhance capacity for monitoring progress by assessing progress periodically.
Recruit interest Optimize relevance, value, and authenticity by clarifying identity.	**Expression and communication** Build fluencies with graduated levels of support for practice and performance by providing for flexible expression options.

WHAT DO WE DO NOW?

If you are intrigued by what the UDL implementation process offers, read on. Steps to consider now include these:

1. **Form your leadership team.** If you haven't created your implementation leadership team, now is the time to do it. Remember to include individuals who are (1) critical to making decisions that can impact your entire system, (2) influential in disseminating information about UDL implementation, and (3) interested teachers who are willing to engage in a multiyear transformation. Throughout your UDL journey continue to ask, "Who else needs to be here?" This will help ensure that you are continually refreshing and strengthening your UDL implementation team.

2. **Start with who and why.** If you haven't identified your system's identity and core values, reviewing Chapter 2. "Spotlight 2.1: Who Are We?" will provide one way to determine your system's core values and need for change.

3. **Anticipate systemic barriers.** Examine how your system currently addresses change with an eye toward identifying those barriers in process, procedures, or perspectives that might get in your way.

4. **Build a strength-based foundation.** To ground your work with a positive foundation, focus now on what makes you strong. Review and analyze available data to discover the expertise that already exists within your system. Understanding your strengths creates a solid base for constructing new knowledge, skills, and practices.

Strategies for identifying your system's strength-based foundation are described in Spotlight 3.1.

SPOTLIGHT 3.1:
What Is Our Foundation?

A discussion about what needs to change can often be deficit-based because it targets weaknesses. The following exercise helps your team focus on what is strong rather than what is wrong. You may choose to have an open-ended brainstorming discussion of your system's strengths, or you may use the list of reflection questions to guide your discussion. Whichever approach you use, be sure to capture what your team uncovers.

Brainstorming Session

1. Ask your leadership group to review the description of your system's identity and core values that you developed for Spotlight 2.1. Think about what *strengths* emerge from your system's identity and core values. These attributes form a positive foundation for your UDL project.

2. Brainstorm a list of cultural or community assets, individuals and their skills, structures, and processes that are evidence of what your system already does well. For example, if a safe learning environment was identified as one of your system's core values, perhaps a strong school-police/safety officer partnership or an effective positive behavioral support program (PBS/PBIS) supports it.

   Use Table 3.2 to guide your discussion.

TABLE 3.2: What's Our Foundation?

STRENGTH ATTRIBUTE	PEOPLE AND SKILL RESOURCE(S)	CULTURAL/ COMMUNITY ASSETS	SUPPORTIVE PROCESSES/ STRUCTURES
Example: Safe learning environment	Example: Ms. Hernandez, PBS lead	Example: School-police safety partnership	Example: Positive Behavior Supports program

Strength-based reflection questions

1. What works well in our system? Name at least five successes.

2. To what extent do things going well depend upon forces within our control?

3. In what ways have we each (individually) supported things that are going well?

4. Who else has contributed to the things that are going well?

5. What do you like to do most? What is most rewarding? What makes it enjoyable to you?

6. What's easy to do? Why?

7. What aspects of our system make us proud? What are our key achievements? What helped them to happen?

8. What obstacles or challenges have we overcome? What contributed to our success?

9. How can we best describe our strengths and successes?

10. What resources found inside and outside of our system, such as community programs, expertise, funding sources, or equipment, contribute to our strengths and successes?

(ADAPTED FROM ATKINS, 2013)

ESSENTIAL QUESTIONS

1. Who's missing? Who's not here and should be involved? How can we entice educators in our system to join us?

2. What are the strengths of our leadership and classroom educators? What do we do really well?

3. How could UDL implementation build upon the good things we're doing?

WHAT'S NEXT? Chapter 4 describes the Explore phase of the UDL implementation process.

SECTION II

Implementation from Explore to Optimize

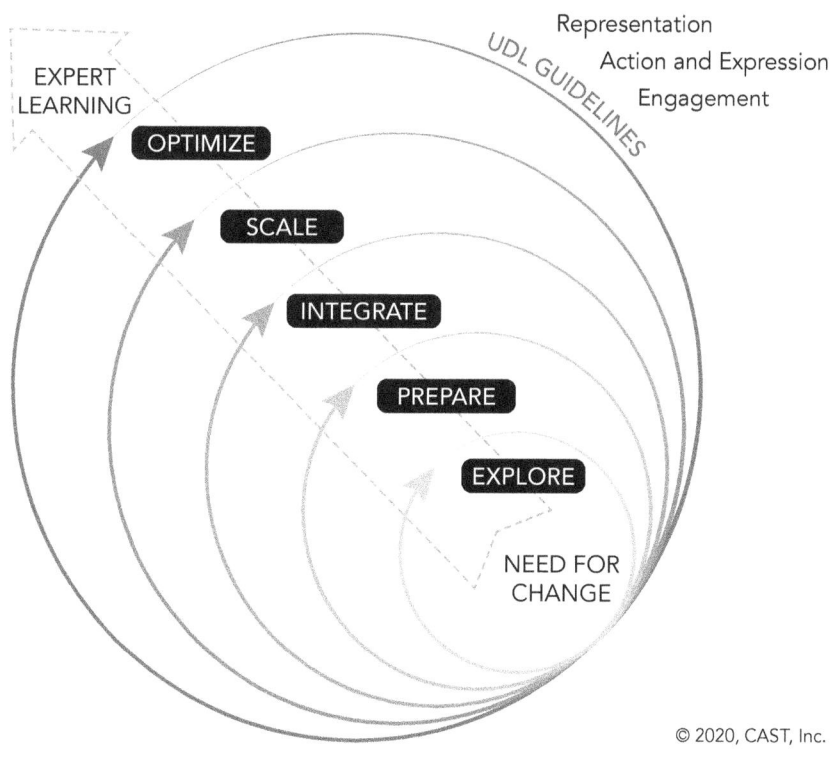

4

Explore

GUIDING QUESTIONS

- What do we need to know to make an informed decision?
- How do we know if we're ready?

LET'S HEAR FROM THE ACCESS PROJECT AT THE UNIVERSITY OF DELAWARE'S CENTER FOR DISABILITIES STUDIES (UD CDS).

The Adapting Curriculum and Classroom Environments for Student Success (ACCESS) Project at the University of Delaware is contracted by the Delaware Department of Education to provide professional learning opportunities to Delaware educators. The project grew out of a need to support academic instruction for students with significant intellectual disabilities, but the focus quickly expanded to include supports that would assist educators with providing accessible and meaningful instruction for all students attending Delaware public schools. ACCESS has been providing educators with statewide, introductory workshops on Universal Design for Learning (UDL) since its inception, viewing UDL as a framework that could be used to help meet the needs of all students, but they struggled with how to deepen their own understanding of UDL and its implementation. As part of their exploration, ACCESS team members began researching and reading (for example, see Meyer et al., 2014). They attended

CAST's Presenter's Institute and the 2016 Summer Symposium, where they connected with others implementing UDL (ACCESS Project team interview, October 2018).

Shortly thereafter, the ACCESS team was asked by the Delaware Department of Education (DDOE) to provide assistance to the Alexis I. DuPont Middle School (AIMS) in Wilmington, Delaware, which was categorized as a focus school based on its performance on Delaware's state assessment. They met with the school's first-year principal; looked at the assessment results, the school's demographics, and other initiatives that were already present in the school; and determined UDL was what was needed to change teacher practices and address variability within the school. The school has a student body of approximately 50% Hispanic/Latino, 28% African American, 19% white, 1% American Indian, 1% Asian, and 1% Multiracial, and in 2015–2016, its proficiency on statewide assessments initially measured at 14% or less in math and English language arts.

The ACCESS team decided to look into UDL as a potential framework for system-wide curriculum design and decision-making. The team connected with Shannon Shultz and her team from Fond du Lac, Wisconsin, who were implementing a district-wide UDL observation and coaching protocol with teachers. The ACCESS team traveled to Fond du Lac to observe UDL implementation and coaching in several schools.

ACCESS returned to AIMS and proposed to Principal Susan Huffman that the school conduct a UDL pilot similar to Fond du Lac's. ACCESS emphasized the importance of getting volunteers for the pilot, and they were able to recruit three seventh grade English language arts teachers. In 2017, ACCESS began a 10-week pilot that consisted of classroom observations, modeling of lessons, planning, and coaching. (The school benefited from tools and resources already developed and shared by Fond du Lac.) Teachers incorporated the UDL Guidelines into their planning and instruction and indicators of student engagement became more evident over the 10-week period. Pilot data persuaded school leadership to expand the initiative to include all English language arts teachers the following year (2017–2018). During that year, teachers planned lessons using the UDL framework and engaged with ACCESS team members in a cycle of observation, reflection, coaching, peer-to-peer observation, and revision. Use of the UDL framework became more prevalent in lesson planning and classroom instruction.

Today, ACCESS team members participate in AIMS's Building Leadership Team (BLT) meetings where a new mission and vision for the school has been developed and aligned to the purpose of UDL. Because of the adoption of a new math curriculum, a math instructional coach was hired for the school with the idea that the ACCESS team would collaboratively work with the coach to apply the UDL framework. UDL lead teachers were also identified. Additional planning time was built into their schedules so teachers could begin observing their peers and providing support on a bimonthly basis. In addition, a UDL book study and visits to Bartholomew Consolidated School Corporation (Indiana) and Baltimore County Public Schools (Maryland) were infused into their UDL professional development plan. As of this writing, the team continues to build awareness among statewide leaders and educators about UDL implementation (see Table 4.2, later in this chapter).

EXPLORE

Like ACCESS team members, your UDL journey begins with the Explore phase. During this phase, you will

- *Assess readiness* by determining interest and willingness to apply UDL as an implementation process.

- *Investigate UDL* as a potential framework for system-wide curriculum design and decision-making.

- *Build awareness* about UDL among key decision makers within and outside of your system.

By the end of the Explore phase, you should know whether you and your core implementation team want to pursue adopting the UDL framework as a systemic process of change.

EXPLORE
- Assess Readiness
- Investigate UDL
- Build Awareness

> **ENGAGEMENT** Assess readiness by determining interest and willingness to apply UDL as an implementation process.

Readiness

Let's first clarify what *readiness* means. Implementation researchers define readiness as a "developmental point at which a person, organization, or system has the capacity and willingness to engage in a particular activity" (Fixsen, Blase, Horner, & Sugai, 2009, p. 1). In other words, readiness exists when individual educators

- concur with your system's identity and core values,
- envision the same desired future,
- recognize the need for change,
- believe that change will make a difference, and
- are willing to change their practice.

Readiness is a critical characteristic within your system that needs to be attended to, nurtured, and developed.

Developing Readiness May Take Time

As you evaluate your system's readiness, it's important to determine if educators (1) concur with the system's identity and core values, (2) agree that there is a need for change, and (3) envision the same desired future. Keep in mind that everyone in your system doesn't need to exhibit equally strong readiness and commitment in the beginning (Novick, Kress, & Elias, 2002). True to the UDL perspective, variability is likely.

Although a certain number of individuals may be ready to engage in implementing UDL early on (so-called *early adopters*), some will need more information to decide if they want to take the "risk" of leaving the relatively private confines of their classrooms and, as Wheelock (2000) says, "go public" with their teaching practice. For example, ACCESS piloted their first UDL implementation project with three volunteers. A high level of trust and professional respect is necessary to entice educators into a project that requires them to potentially acknowledge their professional shortcomings. They will need time to explore what UDL will mean for them and how it could potentially affect them before volunteering. Allow time for professional reflection.

> *All things are ready, if our mind be so.*
> —WILLIAM SHAKESPEARE, from *Henry V*

In addition, the need for change must be significant enough to warrant the work that UDL implementation will take. Evaluating your system's current reality (described in Chapter 3) before you proceed with your UDL implementation plans can not only identify who is interested in and willing to be part of your core UDL implementation team, but it will also help you avoid ineffective efforts and potentially expensive errors.

WATCH FOR UDL

Engagement

- Optimize individual choice and autonomy.
- Optimize relevance, value, and authenticity.
- Minimize threats and distractions.

Both Willingness and Interest Are Essential

According to Jeff Diedrich, cofounder of the UDL Implementation and Research Network (UDL-IRN), willingness and interest are *essential* to your implementation success (National Center on Universal Design for Learning, 2012). When you read this book, you illustrate your interest in UDL implementation. However, you will not be successful if you decide to walk this road alone. You need a committed group or team—that is, a critical mass of early adopters—to join you. As you develop an understanding of who is interested in and willing to make this journey, you will find early adopters who are intrigued by the potential of UDL implementation and eager to become members of your core UDL implementation team.

> *People do not decide to become extraordinary.*
> *They decide to accomplish extraordinary things.*
>
> —EDMUND HILLARY, mountaineer

Frankly, willingness is a characteristic that goes both ways (Cashman et al., 2014). No one wants to join an initiative that is directed by an individual or a group of leaders who are inflexible or impervious to others' ideas. As you proceed, be sure to model your own willingness to probe alternatives, respect variability, accept feedback, strive for continuous improvement, and learn with your team. UDL implementation is a learning process for everyone.

MAKE IT ACTIONABLE Conduct a survey of staff focused on their instructional knowledge, practice, and beliefs, or ask them to engage in an exploratory discussion about their willingness to change their practice and interest in UDL. Refer to "What Do We Do Now" later in this chapter for suggested techniques. Use the results as evidence of your starting point and to measure your progress.

ACTION AND EXPRESSION Investigate UDL as a potential framework for system-wide curriculum design and decision-making.

Investigate

You've already begun your investigation of UDL implementation by reading this book. One of your first tasks is to learn as much as you can about the UDL framework and establish a way that your core implementation team members can do the same. Brainstorm aspects that core team members want to learn more about. Identify potential investigative questions aligned with your system's stated mission or existing initiatives, such as these:

- How does UDL enhance inclusive learning environments?
- How do positive behavior supports (PBS) or multitiered systems of support (MTSS) align with UDL?
- In what ways does our evaluation system align with UDL?

Core team members can then take responsibility to explore specific topics and report back to the rest of the group. Provide multiple ways to represent and share the new knowledge core team members discover.

Respect Variability

Offer a variety of ways that your core team members can learn about UDL implementation. Although most will be eager to participate in a UDL book study group, a couple may prefer to do an individual examination and report their findings to the group. Others will learn best from UDL implementers they meet at a conference or summit focused on UDL. Some may choose to interact with UDL implementers in an online setting, using social media such as Twitter or participating in a webinar or online course, whereas a few may want to visit sites that are already implementing UDL. While you investigate UDL as an overarching curriculum design and decision-making framework, look for examples of UDL implementation in systems like yours.

It may be premature at this point to contract with a UDL consultant, especially if a decision to implement UDL system-wide as a change process has not yet been made. If you do decide that hiring a UDL consultant is the best way for you and your core implementation team to learn about UDL, check to be sure that she not only knows UDL but is also knowledgeable about systems change. If you're looking for a long-term UDL implementation facilitator, ask if the consultant is willing to serve as an implementation guide and not just a presenter.

> **MAKE IT ACTIONABLE** Establish a mechanism for sharing the growing UDL knowledge of core implementation team members. For example, create a web page to serve as a repository for what your core team learns about UDL implementation. Padlet.com works well, is easy to use, and is free. Explore this padlet—*https://padlet.com/eberquist/UDL1*—to discover one way to curate beginning UDL implementation resources. This site focuses on the what, why, and how of UDL and is ideal for a system just beginning to move from theory to practice. Add to it as new information is uncovered and make it available to all members of the core team.

As core UDL implementation team members uncover answers to their investigative questions about the UDL framework and UDL implementation, they can represent their new knowledge in a variety of ways including these:

- A semantic map that is accessible to all members of the core UDL implementation team.

- A more conventional knowledge matrix may work as a repository for your core UDL implementation team. Table 4.1 illustrates a format that you can use as is or adapt to best meet your needs.

TABLE 4.1: UDL Knowledge Matrix Template

INVESTIGATIVE QUESTION	NEW KNOWLEDGE	EVIDENCE SOURCE	TEAM MEMBER
Example: How does our teacher-evaluation system align with UDL?	**Example:** The teacher-evaluation system consistently aligns with UDL, especially in areas related to engaging students and offering flexibility, choice, and scaffolds.	**Example:** Crosswalk between UDL and Danielson Framework; see *https://education.ky.gov/educational/diff/Documents/FFT_UDL_Crosswalk.pdf*	**Example:** Ms. Hernandez

RECOGNITION Build awareness about UDL among key decision makers within and outside of your system.

Build Awareness

From the beginning of your UDL journey, you'll want to build an ever-increasing group of decision makers who understand what you are attempting to do and why it will make a difference. To raise awareness about UDL as an implementation framework, explore who, what, why, and how:

Who: Identify the key decision makers who will make decisions about funding, staff time, professional learning opportunities, curriculum revision, and instructional practices. Who are the individuals that determine what the educators in your system do, how they spend their time, what instructional strategies they use, and how and when they learn about new initiatives? Who are the leaders that can influence others because they are respected by a majority of educators or community members; who can find shortcuts because they are familiar with how things work; or who can help you avoid roadblocks because they know the unwritten rules? Think about including department heads, union leaders, and influential parent and community members.

What: Determine what your system's decision makers need to know about UDL and the implementation process to be adequately equipped to make judgments that will impact your efforts. What questions will they ask about time, funding, and changes in practice? What outcomes will they want to see?

Why: Ascertain as best as you can why your system's decision makers might view UDL implementation as a solution to current problems of practice or system-wide needs. What motivates their decisions? Typical motivations include

- popularity of idea, e.g., *"Lots of important people are interested in implementing UDL."*
- budget-saving aspects, e.g., *"By implementing UDL, we can save money."*
- evidence of effectiveness, e.g., *"Reports show UDL to be effective."*
- linkage to civil or human rights, e.g., *"UDL implementation increases access for all learners."*

How: Define how you can efficiently educate your system's decision makers about those aspects of UDL that are most relevant to your implementation goals. Expecting busy leaders to allot full days at professional learning sessions may be unrealistic and result in disappointment. How can you effectively share what UDL is and how it can enhance learner performance or learning environments in a half-hour meeting or a 15-minute presentation?

> *Awareness is like the sun. When it shines on things, they are transformed.*
>
> —THICH NHAT HANH, Buddhist monk and peace activist

MAKE IT ACTIONABLE You may want to develop a logic model to guide your awareness-building efforts. According to Novak and Rodriguez (2016), constructing a logic model for your UDL implementation initiative serves as a tool for outlining your work. As you define your logic model, you clarify your underlying assumptions, actionable questions, presumed actions, and desired outcomes. A well-constructed logic model provides a way to evaluate your investigative and awareness-building activities. It can also form a base for creating your UDL implementation action plan once a decision is made to implement UDL as your systems change process.

You may prefer to develop a preliminary action plan that includes steps for introducing UDL to identified stakeholders or key audience(s). Different from a logic plan, an action plan determines specific target goals and assigns responsibility for each action. In other words, it guides you in defining *what* your goal is and what steps (i.e., objectives) you need to take, *who* will do what, and *how* and *when* you will measure completion. Look to Chapter 5 to find a template for your UDL implementation action plan.

WHISTLE-STOP If you'd like to know more about developing logic models for your UDL implementation project, see *Universally Designed Leadership: Applying UDL to Systems and Schools* (Novak and Rodriguez, 2016).

WHAT DO WE DO NOW?

Action steps to consider doing now include the following.

Assess Readiness: Determine Interest and Willingness

In addition to directly approaching individuals you know and asking them to join your UDL journey, you can also identify potential core UDL implementation team members while simultaneously determining interest and willingness among your staff. Here are three suggested strategies: (1) complete a 3-2-1 interview process, (2) conduct a staff survey, or (3) engage in a structured dialogue session.

3-2-1 Assessment   After introducing the UDL framework to your staff in a presentation or series of professional learning sessions, consider asking them to complete a 3-2-1 assessment such as the following:

- List three (3) things you learned about UDL that help you decide whether to pursue applying UDL to your instruction.

- Name two (2) key motivators that will encourage you to apply UDL to your practice and support your implementation of UDL.

- Identify one (1) distinct challenge or need that UDL might help you address.

Although the 3-2-1 assessment will not yield a deep understanding of your staff members' willingness and interest in implementing UDL as a change process, analyzing their answers will give you a starting point for developing readiness among them.

Staff Survey   Two sample surveys were developed by CAST during the Gates-funded UDL implementation project: (a) UDL Knowledge, Beliefs, and Practice survey, and (b) UDL Implementation Willingness and Interest survey. They can provide valuable evidence about how your staff views instruction, change, and UDL. Consider conducting them as pre- and post-measurements for your initial UDL implementation efforts. Both surveys are included in the "Resources" section at the end of this book.

Another technique is to conduct staff interviews. In Chapter 3, we shared that the leadership team of the Algonquin Lakeshore Catholic School District Board (Canada) engaged in focused interviews to determine current conceptions of school leadership related to two of the foundations of UDL: learner variability and inclusive practice. See Chapter 3 for more details.

Structured Dialogue Using structured dialogue is another way to assess willingness and interest. Structured dialogue (also referred to as structured dialogic design) is a large-group conversational protocol that seeks to build consensus agreement on complex issues (Giotis, 2012). The process instills respect by valuing and accepting all answers. It involves presenting an open-ended question such as "How do we meet the needs of all learners?" to a group of educators, then generating a multitude of responses and analyzing the results. Responses are categorized, organized, explored, explained, and connected to expose underlying assumptions and beliefs.

Sometimes, it's best to discuss foundational ideas without formally introducing the UDL framework. As a matter of fact, UDL doesn't need to even be mentioned initially. However, by utilizing structured dialogue, a skilled facilitator can help your staff understand how the UDL framework can assist them to better address the learning needs of their students by linking UDL implementation to the staff's own questions and perspectives. You'll recall that in Chapter 2, you read about how the Ysleta Independent School District began their exploration of UDL with a focus on variability. Their leadership team focused on the need to plan for learner variability in advance and brought forward this concept of proactive planning to address learning challenges before the UDL framework was introduced.

The protocol outlined in Spotlight 4.1 requires each person in a group to individually respond to a triggering question; then the group collectively integrates and organizes responses by topics that reflect big ideas, such as responsibility, instruction, learners, assessment, resources, and so on. Typically, an alignment with UDL is discovered as the categories are reviewed. Ultimately, the group sorts topics and responses into items that UDL addresses and those that it doesn't and is positioned to determine whether or not UDL implementation is something they are interested in and willing to pursue.

SPOTLIGHT 4.1: Who's with Me?

UDL Structured Dialogue Protocol

1. Convene group. Explain that their purpose is to focus on instruction and discuss aspects that are of critical importance to them as educators who care about learners.

2. Frame and present an open-ended triggering question, such as "How can we meet the needs of our learners?"

3. Each participant writes their responses to the triggering question on individual notes or Post-it sheets that can be adhered to a large blank sheet of chart paper. Instruct participants to offer one idea or response per sheet so that they can be sorted and organized later.

4. After all responses have been collected on the large chart paper, ask participants to quietly review them and focus on clarifying their meaning. Instruct participants that this is not the time to evaluate responses or determine if they agree or disagree with the responses.

5. Ask participants to identify any response that is unclear to them and offer the opportunity to its author to clarify its meaning.

6. Seek volunteers to join the facilitator(s) in organizing the responses into groupings or categories. It's best to do this task during a break or while participants are engaged in a different activity.

7. Review resulting categories and any outlying items that do not fit within any specific category. Ask participants to either identify a category for the outliers or agree by consensus that the outliers do not belong to any of the defined categories. **Note:** In this situation, consensus does not mean total agreement but instead means that participants do not strongly disagree. Categories may be combined by consensus. There should be at least five categories to offer a choice in the next step.

8. Each participant receives the same number of colored dots, stars, or checkmarks made with markers or other visible indicators. Ask participants to use these indicators to vote on the categories in order of the level of importance each item holds to them individually. For example, participants could allot up to three colored dots to those categories most important to them or they could allot one vote to each category of importance and omit voting on those items that are not important to them. The purpose of this step is to rank the importance of the categories. Therefore, how the votes are allotted depends on how many participants and how many categories you have. Choose a method that will cause the participants to set priorities.

9. Rank the categories from those that received the most to those that received the least number of votes.

10. Assuming at least a basic understanding of UDL, ask participants to sort the identified categories into those that can be addressed by UDL and those that can't.

11. Discuss briefly how UDL implementation can help the participants address the triggering question and their resulting items of concern. Then ask if they are willing to make a commitment to learning more about UDL.

After the structured dialogue session, your core UDL implementation team should review the results and determine if sufficient evidence of willingness and interest in UDL implementation was uncovered.

Investigate UDL

With your core UDL implementation team, brainstorm key questions you want to answer and what aspects of UDL you want to explore. Clarify how your team members will share their new knowledge about UDL with each other. A plethora of resources about UDL are available and more are being added all the time.

Build Awareness

Begin building your network by identifying potential stakeholders who may consider joining a cross-stakeholder task force. Typically, cross-stakeholders are not employees of your system. They could include non-staff decision makers such as board members, parents, and business and community leaders. These individuals can help build a shared foundation of understanding and increase interest among important decision-making bodies, funding organizations, and community groups. They can also share in your successes as your implementation project progresses. Determine how to best present information about UDL to them. An important initial task is the development of commonly understood vocabulary and terminology associated with UDL implementation. As your UDL project proceeds, a common language makes sharing information easier.

As mentioned earlier in this chapter, Delaware's ACCESS Project team continues to build awareness of UDL among key decision makers within and outside of their system. Table 4.2 illustrates the organized manner they used to accomplish this.

TABLE 4.2: ACCESS Project Outreach

STATE LEADERSHIP	DELAWARE EDUCATORS	OUT-OF-STATE
Office of Innovation and School Improvement • Wilmington schools	Statewide professional development workshops (Introduction and Advanced)	Association of University Centers on Disabilities (AUCD) 2017 poster presentation
Office of Curriculum and Instruction • Literacy cadre meetings	District presentations	Association for Supervision and Curriculum Development (ASCD) Empower 18 poster presentation
Office of Assessment • UDL and instruction aligned to alternate assessment standards	UDL focus at Delaware's Inclusion Conference 2018	CAST 2017 UDL Summer Symposium presentation
Community Advisory Council (CAC) presentations	University of Delaware's Center for Disciplinary Studies (UD CDS) Lunchtime for Learning presentations	UDL-Implementation and Research Network attendance with UDL leads from Alexis I. DuPont Middle School (2017–18 SY)
Goals related to UDL implementation part of the CDS's five-year strategic plan • UDL embedded across CDS initiatives	Continued UDL focus at Delaware's Inclusion Conference 2019	21st Century Community Learning presentation

STATE LEADERSHIP	DELAWARE EDUCATORS	OUT-OF-STATE
UDL embedded across ACCESS initiatives	UDL embedded across UD • Preservice teachers' coursework • Guest lecturers • UD Lab School presentations	

When the awareness of what is achievable brushes your life, your journey has begun.

—LORII MYERS, entrepreneur

ESSENTIAL QUESTIONS

1. What can we learn from others who are engaged in implementing the UDL framework?

2. Why do you view UDL implementation as a change or transformative process?

3. As you explore UDL implementation, what benefits do you foresee and what challenges worry you?

4. In what ways will other local/state/national initiatives or frameworks align with UDL?

5. In the past, what successful strategies have you used for raising awareness about new programs or initiatives? What are some pitfalls to avoid?

6. In terms of readiness, what areas will need the focus of your attention: personnel, resources, curriculum?

WHAT'S NEXT? Chapter 5 describes the Prepare phase of the UDL implementation process.

5

Prepare

GUIDING QUESTIONS

- How accepting is our learning environment climate?
- How can we leverage what we're already doing to prepare for UDL implementation?
- What do we want to accomplish?

LET'S HEAR FROM THE OCONOMOWOC AREA SCHOOL DISTRICT (OASD) IN WISCONSIN.

OASD serves just over 5,000 students and is committed to providing all children with high-quality, engaging, and personalized learning experiences. Their district vision is grounded in seven non-negotiables:

1. All learners will be held to high expectations.
2. All learners will succeed.
3. All teachers will collaborate to strengthen each other's effectiveness.
4. All teachers teach all learners.
5. All individual learner needs will be met in the general education environment through flexible learning experiences.

6. All learners will engage in relevant curriculum that is diverse.

7. All teachers will design instruction by knowing each individual.

As the district leadership worked to operationalize these non-negotiables, they began to explore the UDL framework. UDL appealed to the district team because of its foundations in social justice and evidence-based practices. To extend their understanding of UDL, they connected with staff at CAST, attended the UDL institute at the Harvard Graduate School of Education, and visited the Bartholomew Consolidated School Corporation (BCSC) in Indiana (see Chapter 8 for more information on BCSC). These learning experiences prompted them to begin to make some structural changes in OASD to enhance the learning environment climate and better reflect their already-existing commitment to addressing learner variability. Actions included teaching staff to use person-first language, committing to coteaching, and changing the title of special education teachers to learning strategists. They describe how educators' roles changed in this way:

> *The learning strategists and teaching and learning team really came together . . . lines were blurred, and the learning strategist became part of the fabric of planning. They specialize in a grade or content area, so they have knowledge of the curriculum; they receive textbooks, professional development and attend all curriculum meetings; they are completely integrated into content or grade level teams, K–12 (OASD team interview, June 2018).*

After almost three years of working to build this inclusive conceptual understanding with teachers and leaders, the district leadership team and the superintendent believed that the climate in OASD was ready for the "how" of UDL. They began to identify measurable outcomes and develop an action plan using the plan-do-study-act process. The district identified a UDL team tasked with leading this planning process. In addition, the director of research started a cohort analysis that compared a model UDL classroom to cohorts not engaged in applying UDL to their instruction.

WHISTLE-STOP To learn more about *people-first language,* go to the description offered by The Arc at *https://www.thearc.org/who-we-are/media-center/people-first-language.*

PREPARE

Similar to OASD's actions, once your team decides to pursue systemic UDL implementation, preparations begin. During the Prepare phase, you will

- *create a UDL climate* that respects variability and accepts it as the rule throughout your system,

- conduct a self-reflection assessment to uncover and *map resources* and determine which organizational policies, processes, structures, and practices might need to change, and

- *define measurable outcomes* and an action plan.

During the Prepare phase, you will determine *where* your UDL journey will take you, *what* steps you will need to take, *how* you will measure your progress, *which* resources you already have in place, and which ones you will need to effectively support your UDL journey.

ENGAGEMENT Create a UDL climate that maintains high expectations and accepts variability as the rule rather than the exception.

UDL Climate

The Prepare phase concentrates on laying the groundwork for your UDL implementation initiative by creating a UDL climate for learning. What do we mean by a *UDL climate?* In a work environment, *climate* is usually associated with perceptions and measurable behavioral patterns (Hall & Hord, 2001). The National School Climate Center (NSCC) defines *school climate* as patterns of experiences of students, parents, and school personnel with the school's ". . . norms, goals, values, interpersonal relationships, teaching and learning practices, and organizational structures" (Cohen, 2014, p. 2). For our purposes, let's extend the definition of school climate beyond a school to encompass any learning environment. The Partnership for 21st Century Learning (2020) defines a *learning environment* as a support system that organizes the conditions under which students learn best. They further state that effective instruction occurs within an optimal student-centered learning environment. With this interpretation in mind, a learning environment that exemplifies a UDL climate values the contributions of all learners and reflects the underlying UDL goal that all learners can become expert learners given the scaffolds and supports they need to be successful (Meyer et al., 2014). The description at the beginning of this chapter of how OASD approached initial implementation of UDL is an excellent example of creating a learning climate that is conducive to successful UDL implementation.

> **REFLECTION** How would you describe the climate of your learning environment?

Embed High Expectations for All

Teachers who believe that all students can learn create classrooms and curricula that are welcoming and inclusive. In a UDL climate, it is unacceptable to expect that some learners will reach learning goals and some will not. As Novak (2014) asserts, teachers with high expectations leave no room for failure. A learning environment that reflects a UDL climate accepts the contributions of all learners and sets goals that maintain high expectations.

> *High achievement always takes place in the framework of high expectation.*
>
> —CHARLES F. KETTERING, inventor

Look to your data to determine if educators' preconceived ideas about student potential unwittingly set limitations. You'll find the evidence you need in the educator surveys, inclusion rates, and student performance levels that you analyzed during the Explore phase. If your data suggest that expectations are not uniformly set at high levels for all learners, you will need to provide professional learning sessions focused on changing teacher mindsets.

You'll recall from Chapter 3 that teachers typically transform their instruction based on changes in their beliefs. Transforming attitudes and perspectives is not easy, but it may be where you need to start. Some educators must reexamine their perspectives about their students before they recognize that maintaining high expectations for all is desirable and will lead to expert learning.

MacDonald (2013) describes educators with a *fixed mindset* who work in environments that encourage prejudging, sorting, and labeling of learners based on presumptions about their abilities. Fixed mindsets negatively impact teachers' willingness to change their practice because they don't believe all learners have the potential to learn at high levels. In stark contrast, educators with a *growth mindset* work in environments rooted in the belief that all learners can learn, and that improvement comes from effort, study, and perseverance (MacDonald, 2013).

For teachers to unlearn patterns of behavior that emote low expectations, exclusion, discrimination, or rejection, they will need new knowledge, authentic experiences, and honest self-reflection that helps them to recognize their existing perceptions and misconceptions. In addition, take the time now to examine and eliminate policies, processes, or procedures that support a fixed mindset and replace them with ones that foster a growth mindset among educators. For instance, let's review the example of OASD at the beginning of this chapter. District leaders realized that the titles for special educators encouraged a fixed mindset about what these educators did and who they taught. When their titles were changed and they were moved into more flexible roles, learning specialists (formerly known as special educators) were able to be more engaged with instructional planning for all learners.

Key Concepts Address Mindset

Emphasizing three key concepts in the beginning of the implementation process can hasten a change in educator mindset:

- *The myth of average.* Harvard faculty member Todd Rose has successfully argued in his writings and videos that "... no one is average" (T. Rose, 2016, p. 11). Yet, many teachers aim their instruction at the so-called middle segment of students. This practice ignores the students who function "in the margins." Learners who struggle are written off as unable and the learning needs of students with strengths and talents are neglected because of the misconception that "they will get it on their own." When teachers presume that all learners can achieve given the right scaffolds and supports, individual student performance increases to rigorous levels (Williamson & Blackburn, 2010).

- *Learner variability.* The UDL guidelines represent the aspects of learner variability that exist in every group of learners. Offer teachers the opportunity to develop an understanding of the concept of learner variability by experiencing UDL as learners themselves. Ask them to compare the differences that exist among them as learners. How does each teacher perceive information? How do they react in a stressful or frustrating learning situation? What scaffolds work for them that won't work for others? Authentic experiences can disabuse misconceptions about learning potential. Associated with the concept of learner variability is the concept of *fairness.* Equal access to information is not necessarily fair. Even though teachers may provide every student with the same content or resources, they haven't created a fair learning environment. A *fair learning environment* is one that provides every learner with what he or she needs to be successful (Lavoie, 1989).

- *Expert learning.* The goal of applying UDL to instruction is developing expert learners (Meyer et al., 2014). Expert learners are not students who get all As but those who are knowledgeable, strategic, goal-directed, purposeful, and motivated by the mastery of learning itself (National Center on Universal Design for Learning, 2014). Anyone can become an expert learner. The teacher's role in developing expert learning is to design learning options that remove barriers. Aiming for expert learning will have a powerful transformational impact on the learning environment and create a UDL climate.

You see what you expect to see, Severus.
—DUMBLEDORE FROM J. K. ROWLING'S *HARRY POTTER* SERIES

Debunk the Myths

Both Berquist (2017) and Ralabate (2016) highlight the importance of initially debunking misconceptions about UDL as you address educators' beliefs about their practice. This can occur during the Explore, Prepare, or Integrate phase. Myths that should be refuted include these:

- *UDL is not special education.* Although UDL was originally conceived to provide accessible instruction for students with disabilities, it has evolved beyond that construct. Today, the UDL framework is viewed as a framework you can use to address the learning needs of all learners.

- *UDL is not technology instruction.* Many technology specialists are UDL advocates, which sometimes causes the framework to be misconstrued as requiring technology, particularly digital technology. Digital and other media tools offer accessibility and flexibility but are not necessary for UDL implementation.

- *UDL is not a checklist or set of lesson plans.* Some educators believe that if they offer a few options in their lesson plan, they are "doing" UDL. Offering choice can dramatically enhance lessons, but UDL implementation is more than this. Rather than clicking boxes on a static checklist, applying UDL entails designing learning environments with a proactive mindset or *UDL lens* that permeates how you think about curriculum, instruction, and learning.

> **MAKE IT ACTIONABLE** In addition to conducting the survey of instructional knowledge, practice, and beliefs mentioned in the previous chapter and detailed later in the "Resources" section, you may want to survey staff about their professional development interests and needs during the Prepare phase. Their responses will provide you with insights into existing mindsets and misunderstandings. Bartholomew Consolidated School Corporation (BCSC), a public school district in Columbus, Indiana, developed a short survey of professional development needs, which they permitted CAST to adapt during the Gates-funded UDL implementation project. The Professional Development Needs Assessment survey is available in the "Resources" section.

> **RECOGNITION** Map resources available for UDL implementation, such as personnel, learning material and products, curriculum, professional development, structures, processes, and procedures.

Resource Mapping

A common concern among educators who are implementing UDL is garnering enough time for planning. Changing your practice takes thoughtful planning; and planning takes time. One effective way to ease the burden of time constraints that educators encounter along their UDL journey is to use the collective knowledge of the team to gather or build UDL resources and make these resources available to everyone on the team.

Resource mapping is a strategic process focused on identifying needed resources, cataloging acquired resources, and determining which resources are missing and need to be developed (Sanetti, Kratochwill, Volpiansky, & Ring, 2011). Resources are more than instructional materials and curricula. They include organizational policies, processes, procedures, structures, and practices and may include personnel, programs and services, facilities, technology, and sources of funding. For instance, school leaders who are well-versed in positive behavioral interventions can help team members develop engagement strategies, and media or adaptive technology programs can offer accessibility options. Or, a closet of materials no longer utilized for a defunded program can be repurposed for general classroom use.

As OASD prepared for UDL implementation, they used a mapping process to determine which organizational policies, processes, procedures, and practices might need to change to move their UDL implementation project forward. For example, once they realized the importance of dedicating a position to UDL implementation and coaching, they repurposed existing funds from special education and curriculum and instruction budgets to create UDL coaches for each school. They also revamped the traditional school librarian position into an instructional coach. See Chapter 6 for more details on how OASD realigned their system with their UDL implementation project.

By mapping resources that are available for UDL implementation, your team will know what you have, what you need, and what's available in the larger community. Adapted from Sanetti et al. (2011), the following stages segment resource mapping into four distinct steps:

Who: Prior to creating the resource map for your UDL implementation initiative, the Pre-mapping stage involves designating who is responsible for locating resources. After you identify your cross-stakeholder team to broaden your impact, determine a common language and frame of reference for your team. Clarify the purpose of your resource map, identify where and how it can be accessed, and define communication procedures the mapping team will use.

What: The Mapping stage includes both setting priorities and identifying the types of resources you need. Start by defining a goal or setting priorities to guide your collaborative mapping efforts. Your UDL team should specify categories of resources (e.g., skilled personnel, funding sources, professional development structures, intervention protocols and procedures, curriculum materials, instructional strategies, tools).

Where: The Strategic Implementation stage focuses on collecting and analyzing identified resources and making them available to your UDL implementation team. Strategize how these resources can be applied to tackle potential learning barriers and catalog them so they are conveniently located. To further hone in on UDL implementation, you may want to use the three UDL principles to refine your resource descriptions. In other words, designate resources as supports for engagement, knowledge-building (i.e., representation), or strategic planning or communication (i.e., action and expression). Note any evidence or research of resource effectiveness that you find.

How: The final stage, the Evaluate-Refresh-Recycle stage, is sometimes forgotten but shouldn't be. Set a time when the resource map will be reviewed and updated. It's important to survey team members to evaluate its use and effectiveness. As necessary, revise both the resource map's structure and the process used to create it.

Why Is Resource Mapping Important?

Effective resource mapping helps you to establish a more sustainable UDL implementation project. Like OASD, through resource mapping, your team can identify human as well as material assets that help facilitate, scaffold, and support learning in multiple environments. Your team can avoid duplication and build stronger roots for your project by finding ways to connect your UDL initiative with resources used by existing frameworks or programs. Your team can also save time because many instructional ideas can be applied across classrooms and curriculum areas. Furthermore, sharing resources can encourage team members to learn strategies from each other. By avoiding duplicative efforts spent locating resources, your team can focus on exploring creative ways to apply the UDL framework.

In addition, the process of resource mapping helps uncover existing limitations and gaps in resource availability. Once gaps are established, your team should develop a plan for either accessing or creating the missing assets. This aspect of resource mapping provides your team with the opportunity to create partnerships with community groups who can help your team fill existing gaps.

MAKE IT ACTIONABLE Try Padlet (*www.padlet.com*) or another resource-mapping tool in your UDL implementation project.

WHISTLE-STOP If you'd like to learn more about resource mapping, see Sanetti et al.'s *Resource Mapping: A Tool Kit* (2011), the SWIFT Center's publication *Facilitating Resource Mapping and Matching* (2016), and the National Center on Secondary Education and Transition's *Essential Resources* (2005).

ACTION AND EXPRESSION Define outcomes with measurable outcomes and an action plan.

UDL Implementation Action Plan

During the Prepare phase, you will use what you know about your system to outline measurable outcomes that define the course you will take on your UDL journey. By now, your UDL implementation team should have gathered a lot of data. Remember to build from your data, particularly the strengths that currently exist system-wide, as you develop your action plan.

Where to Start

First, remember that implementing UDL is not the goal of your action plan. Instead, implementing UDL is the strategy you are going to apply to your problem of practice or identified need for change. Now is the time to recall why you want to adopt UDL. What do you want your UDL implementation plan to address? What is it that you feel you can accomplish by implementing UDL?

Your shared vision expresses *why* you are implementing UDL. As discussed in Chapter 3, a key element of a successful UDL initiative is jointly working toward a clear shared vision or mutually desired future. Although your shared vision may be aligned with a school motto, district mission, or your system's strategic vision statement, it probably is not measurable, or it is too general to guide your implementation work. Examples of typical vision statements include *"Provide a challenging, inclusive learning environment for all learners"* or *"Engage all learners in effective, culturally responsive instruction."* Your shared vision can and should represent a lofty ideal, but your UDL implementation action plan needs to be concrete if you want to make your shared vision a reality.

> *Plans are nothing; planning is everything.*
> —PRESIDENT DWIGHT D. EISENHOWER

Define Your SMART Goal

To develop an effective UDL implementation action plan, start by defining measurable outcomes that address your identified need for change and shared vision and include (1) at least one overarching goal and (2) objectives that serve as meaningful stages or steps to achieving your overarching goal(s). Each goal and objective should answer these questions:

1. What do we want to accomplish?

2. When will we accomplish it?

3. How will we know we accomplished it?

Using the SMART acronym to develop your goals and objectives will target your UDL action plan on sustainable change. Many K–12 school teams have learned how to apply the SMART acronym to goal development for school improvement plans in recent years (Conzemius & O'Neill, 2002). Originally introduced to business managers for strategic planning purposes by George Doran (1981), the SMART process for developing goals and objectives offers clarity and measurable specificity to your action plan. According to Ralabate (2016), the following descriptions are most often used by educators for the SMART acronym:

Specific: Goals and objectives clearly state what you expect to accomplish and are easily understood by all team members.

Measurable: Authentic evidence or data are used to measure every goal and objective so that all team members can assess progress toward achievement.

Attainable: Goals and objectives maintain high expectations without being unreasonable or unattainable within the span of your project and the resources available.

Results-oriented: Goals and objectives focus on relevant results that make an observable, meaningful difference for your learners.

Time-bound: Goals and objectives are achievable within the time span of your project.

Hurdles to Avoid

The act of jointly developing SMART goals can be an invigorating learning event for your team. But writing SMART goals and objectives will not guarantee success. MacDonald (2013) points out hurdles that lead to so-called "Seemingly SMART" goals—goals that ". . . look good on paper but don't impact student learning" (p. 85).

To avoid the trap of Seemingly SMART goals and objectives, keep these points in mind as you develop your UDL action plan:

- Your goals should focus on learner outcomes, not on activities or events. Activities are the means to the goal, not the desired measurable outcome. Goals that stipulate that *"teachers will attend X number of professional learning workshops"* or that *"students will participate in X number of counseling sessions"* do not clearly impact learning. Also, outcomes need to be specific to the development of learner skills, not resources or plans.

- Your goals should apply robust, targeted, ongoing measurements. When you develop goals based on insufficient data or measurement requirements, your team is forced to estimate your baseline data, use measurements that don't provide the team with timely information, or rely on arbitrary evaluation tools that don't measure the outcomes targeted by your goal. For example, summative assessments, such as annual standardized assessments, are poor choices for measuring goals. They are typically only snapshots of performance and won't allow for tracking ongoing progress.

- Your goals should be replicable given available, supported resources. It may be impossible to maintain a project once initial funding runs out or personnel working on it are redirected to other tasks. Goals that define unsustainable strategies or one-time-only resources may give you an "initial win" but will not lead to enduring change.

- Your goals should be time-bound within a logical or meaningful timeframe. If your goals extend beyond a natural time period, such as a school year or annual budget cycle, your team can become distracted, disillusioned, or frustrated. Your project runs the risk of losing momentum or focus. If it takes more time than you've got, adjust your goal into incremental targets so that your team can more easily accomplish them within the project's timeframe. If it looks like you might not achieve a goal or objective within your timeframe, reexamine and change the strategy before totally abandoning the goal.

> *A goal without a plan is just a wish.*
> —ANTOINE DE SAINT-EXUPÉRY, author of *The Little Prince*

Table 5.1 illustrates examples of how an identified need for change could align with suggested shared vision statements and SMART goals.

TABLE 5.1: Alignment of Needs, Shared Visions, and SMART Goals

NEED FOR CHANGE	SHARED VISION	EXAMPLES OF SMART GOALS
Data reveal a significant academic gap in reading levels.	Educate our learners to high academic levels in literacy/reading.	By May, a minimum of 85% of students will score a 3 or above on periodic administrations of the District Reading Rubric.
Challenging behavior interferes with learning.	Provide a safe and orderly learning environment.	Office discipline referrals for disrespectful behavior will decrease by 40% by the end of the year.
Few students with disabilities are included or progressing in inclusive general education environments.	All learners, including students with disabilities, have access to and are learning successfully in inclusive general education environments.	By the end of the year, at least 90% of students with disabilities will gain at least a year's growth in reading or math in inclusive general education environments.
Student absences negatively impact teaching and learning.	All learners are inspired to participate and achieve at their highest levels.	Weekly unexcused absences will decrease from 30% to below 15% by June.

Prioritize, Customize, and Infuse Flexibility

As you develop your plan's objectives, prioritize the necessary steps you must take to accomplish your overarching goal(s). UDL implementation plans that infuse the UDL framework into their implementation strategies focus on proactive approaches and build in opportunities for flexibility and choice. They are also nimble enough to allow for revision if the team encounters overwhelming barriers. Think strategically about contingencies that will allow your team to continue their work, such as aligning with other priorities.

You may be tempted to adopt an action plan that another system has used successfully. Don't do it. No one plan works for every system because each system has varying resources and challenges. You certainly can learn from others and adopt strategies others have used, but make certain that your plan is customized to address your system's circumstances.

Monitor and Measure Progress Regularly

As you develop your objectives, make sure they are measurable. Ask *"How will we know we accomplished this?"* for every step. Use an evidence-based approach. Identify what evidence or data sets you will use to evaluate each objective. Be careful not to get caught up in a "factory" mindset that measures inputs and outputs. For example, counting the number of educators who attend workshops or the number of choices that teachers offer in a classroom are measures of inputs and outputs. You want to employ evaluation strategies that assess outcomes and impact, such as improvement in learner engagement and increases in student knowledge. Consistent meetings and scheduled automatic checkpoints will help you to monitor progress and adjust resource allocation, if necessary. Apply innovative strategies including reallocating existing funding, sharing resources, and tweaking responsibilities. Continually mark the progress you're making through scheduled checkpoints.

It's likely that new team members who come on board before you've achieved your goals may advocate for revising the plan or changing course. Offer them other ways they can provide their perspectives and influence the goals rather than scrapping your action plan. Most importantly, take the time to acknowledge growth and celebrate accomplishments.

Design Thinking

Another approach for developing your shared goals and UDL action plan is the *design thinking* model. Originally proposed by experts in the software design and business management fields as a problem-solving process, design thinking has been adapted to tackle a variety of "complex" or "wicked" problems in education (Leverenz, 2014, p. 3). Rather than the familiar analytical process that guides teams to break down problems and develop one course of action, design thinking aims to create innovative solutions through an iterative collaborative process. According to the Design Thinking for Educators Toolkit (IDEO, 2013), the five phases of the design process are

1. **Discovery:** Defining and building a deep understanding of the design challenge
2. **Interpretation:** Transforming educators' stories into meaningful insights
3. **Ideation:** Brainstorming to generate multiple, fresh ideas

4. **Experimentation:** Building prototypes that make the ideas tangible

5. **Evolution:** Developing needed changes and documenting progress over time

Design thinking allows you to take a learning approach to evaluating outcomes of your action plan. These are questions to keep in mind: (1) What do we know? (2) What do we want to learn? (3) How will we apply what we learn to future planning?

Develop a Robust Action Plan

CAST created a prototype of a UDL implementation action plan during the Gates-funded UDL implementation project that includes three main elements at the top: (a) identified need for change, (b) shared vision, and (c) overarching goal. By stating these critical elements on the action plan, you keep them at the forefront of your project's design. Like other action plan formats, the objectives or steps to achieve the goal are defined within the body of the action plan.

Although every system is different, the following four components are usually ones to include when developing an action plan:

- Assigned responsibility (e.g., either specific individuals or teams)
- Strategies or methods
- Resources or incentives needed
- Timeline or deadline (including times for periodic progress monitoring)

> **MAKE IT ACTIONABLE** The first thing you should do after determining your goals is define the specific evidence or data you expect to use to measure your progress and make sure that you have baseline data for each goal and objective. Explore using teacher surveys as pre- and post-evaluations of changes in knowledge and perspectives, and regularly collected data, such as student performance rubrics and assessments that provide valid, ongoing, or formative information. Many free resources are available on the process of creating action plans. For example, the Center for Community Health and Development at the University of Kansas provides easy-to-follow guidelines for strategic planning and a free template in their Community Tool Box (https://ctb.ku.edu/en/table-of-contents/structure/strategic-planning/develop-action-plans/tools).

WHAT DO WE DO NOW?

Steps to consider now include assessing your climate, resource mapping, and developing your UDL action plan. Spotlights 5.1, 5.2, and 5.3 provide detailed guidance.

Assess Your Climate

First, examine the data you gathered during the Explore phase for information associated with your system's climate. If you don't have enough or the right measures, use a survey to determine the knowledge and beliefs of your staff, such as the CAST UDL Knowledge, Beliefs, and Practice survey or the UDL Professional Development Needs Assessment survey, originally developed by the Bartholomew Consolidated School Corporation (BCSC). Both are available in the "Resources" section. Use your analysis of your system's climate to determine the professional learning that may be necessary to build a UDL climate of acceptance and high expectations.

Another way to garner a quick assessment of educators' attitudes toward maintaining high expectations within an inclusive learning environment is to ask teachers to complete a UDL Climate *SWOT analysis*. For the purposes of the SWOT analysis, strengths (S) and weaknesses (W) are considered factors that are within our control. Opportunities (O) and threats (T), usually presented by external forces, can be anticipated but are typically outside of our control. Compile the results of the SWOT analysis looking for patterns that point to common beliefs about expectations and learner performance. For an example of a UDL Climate SWOT Analysis, see Spotlight 5.1.

Complete Your Resource Map

Meet with your team to decide how you will create your resource map. If you'd like to use a template created with UDL in mind, consider using the resource mapping process described in Spotlight 5.2.

Define Your UDL Implementation Action Plan

At this point, your team should have enough baseline data and information about what is needed to develop your project's action plan. If you'd like to use a template that's focused on UDL implementation, check out Spotlight 5.3.

SPOTLIGHT 5.1:
Are We Prepared? A UDL Climate SWOT Analysis

Directions

Think about your current learning environment. List two to three items in response to the questions listed in each area. Strengths and weaknesses are defined as internal factors that are within your control. Opportunities and threats are external factors that can be anticipated but are not within your control.

STRENGTHS What **assets and skills** influence learner expectations and performance?	**WEAKNESSES** What **deficits and needs** influence learner expectations and performance?
OPPORTUNITIES What external factors **benefit** learner expectations and performance?	**THREATS** What external factors **interfere** with learner expectations and performance?

SPOTLIGHT 5.2:
What Do We Have and What Do We Need?

Remember to include the following in your resource map:

- Contact person for the item
- Brief description
- Where to find it (e.g., location, online link)
- Limitations of who can use it (e.g., age/grade levels, curriculum areas) and copyright issues, if any
- Costs, if any
- Accessibility options, including alternate formats

Instructions for how to insert or add items to the resource map should be straightforward.

Example of a UDL Resource Map

RESOURCE	CONTACT	UDL PRINCIPLE(S)	DESCRIPTION	LOCATION/ LINK	LIMITATION	COSTS	ACCESSIBILITY
Example: Formative assessment	**Example:** Martin	**Example:** Engagement Action & Expression	**Example:** Quick classroom assessment techniques	**Example:** 1. List on Padlet & available from instructional leads 2. See George Washington University*	**Example:** OK for all grades; List is best for middle school, high school, college	**Example:** None	**Example:** Check for digital and alternate formats as needed
Example: Inspiration	**Example:** Maria	**Example:** Representation	**Example:** Concept mapping tool	**Example:** www.inspiration.com	**Example:** Uses Windows 7 or Macintosh OS X 10.7 and later For Grades 6–Adult	**Example:** Site license can be purchased Individual subscription = $39.95	**Example:** Supports keyboard accessibility options

* https://library.gwu.edu/utlc/teaching/assessment-student-learning

SPOTLIGHT 5.3: What's Our Plan?

Identified need for change: _____

Shared vision: _____

SMART Goal: _____

OBJECTIVE	RESPONSIBILITY	STRATEGIES	RESOURCES	EVIDENCE	TIMELINE

ESSENTIAL QUESTIONS

1. What challenges do we anticipate in preparing for UDL implementation? How do we plan to address these challenges?

2. How accessible and flexible is our learning environment?

3. To what extent do we need to make changes that will create an accepting climate for UDL implementation?

4. What data do we need? How will data be used to measure our progress?

5. What resources, procedures, and structures do we need to implement UDL effectively?

6. How will we identify necessary supports and resources? Which ones are critical to success?

7. How will we celebrate and share our successes?

WHAT'S NEXT? Chapter 6 describes the Integrate phase of the UDL implementation process.

6

Integrate

GUIDING QUESTIONS

- How can fostering a collaborative environment enhance our work?
- What are the most effective options for developing educator expertise?
- What system-wide priorities and infrastructure will support UDL implementation?

LET'S HEAR FROM BALTIMORE COUNTY PUBLIC SCHOOLS (BCPS).

In the UDL field, most of the work has been focused on using UDL to design flexible learning environments in pre-K–20 environments. Although this is crucially important, it is also time to consider how this research-based framework can and should move beyond classroom design and into the design of professional learning for adults. In addition to using UDL as a framework for instructional design, Baltimore County Public Schools (BCPS), in Maryland, uses UDL as a framework for empowering adult learners to make decisions. Throughout this chapter, you will hear from Billy Burke, Baltimore County's Chief of Organizational Effectiveness about how BCPS has implemented UDL throughout the Integrate phase, including using the UDL lens to reimagine the design of professional learning.

INTEGRATE

The cornerstone of the Integrate phase is building capacity and system-wide policies, processes, procedures, and practices that will help you put your UDL implementation action plan into operation. Consequently, pathways during the Integrate phase address

- *fostering collaboration* to hasten the infusion of UDL into learning environments;

- *developing educator expertise* by providing customized professional learning opportunities, including UDL-infused professional development workshops, professional learning communities (PLCs), and coaching; and

- *evaluating* the efficacy of established policies, processes, and procedures, inserting the UDL principles as needed and *creating* new practices that align with the UDL framework.

ENGAGEMENT Foster collaboration to support and hasten infusion of UDL into learning environments.

Collaboration

Collaboration is defined as "the process of . . . working together to complete a task or achieve a goal" (see *https://en.wikipedia.org/wiki/Collaboration*). It is often expected in today's learning environments (Santamaria & Thousand, 2004). In fact, for more than three decades, professional collaboration among educators has been heralded as a powerful tool and mandatory precursor for successful learner outcomes (Hall & Hord, 2001; A. Hargreaves, 1994; Little, 1982; Mattatall & Power, 2018). Though it might seem pedantic to critique aspects of fostering collaboration as you begin the Integrate phase of your UDL implementation initiative, it is timely to do so. There are hazards ahead if you assume collaboration exists when it really doesn't.

Collaboration vs. Coercion

According to A. Hargreaves (1994), there is a negative impact when educators are coerced into involuntary circumstances that attempt to mimic team collaboration without appropriating enough time and building necessary skills. Unchecked, two results—inflexibility and inefficiency—can doom a project aimed at transforming instruction. To learn more, look at Table 6.1, which illustrates A. Hargreaves' (1994) key distinctions between the desirable context of collaboration and the debilitating consequences of what he called "contrived collegiality."

TABLE 6.1: Collaboration Compared to Contrived Collegiality

COLLABORATION	CONTRIVED COLLEGIALITY
Spontaneous	Administratively regulated
Collaborative working relationships are administratively supported and allowed to evolve.	Meeting times and work products are imposed.
Voluntary	Compulsory
Productive relationships derive from their perceived value among educators.	Working together is required or indirectly imposed by veiled threats or promises of advancement.
Development oriented	Implementation oriented
Commitment to a common goal is obvious. Educators purposely develop products of their own initiative.	Educators are required to implement the mandates of others.

COLLABORATION	CONTRIVED COLLEGIALITY
Pervasive across time and space Scheduled meetings are not the only times for working together. Unregulated, informal sharing permeates the learning environment.	Fixed in time and space Scheduled meetings are planned and regulated by administrative decisions. Use of planning time is mandated and controlled.
Unpredictable Outcomes are teacher generated. Educators exert discretion over how the curriculum is delivered.	Predictable Outcomes are closely controlled by administration. Planning feels scripted or inflexible.

(Adapted from A. Hargreaves [1994])

Although A. Hargreaves (1994) did not specifically examine UDL implementation, three pertinent lessons can be gleaned from his research:

1. Teachers should be empowered to make decisions about how they will apply UDL to their practice.

2. Collaboration requires a common goal.

3. Administrative support (especially in terms of creating time and space to work together) is necessary but administrative mandates are detrimental.

Recruit Rather Than Select

As discussed in Chapter 4, it's unwise to assume that every teacher is interested in changing his or her practice. Similarly, collaboration is not always instinctual. Consequently, joining your collaborative team should be a choice, not an assignment. This means that soliciting volunteers is better than conscripting unwilling group members.

The data you collected during the Explore phase will offer insights into who will engage voluntarily in your project. But to pique interest, you may need to market your UDL implementation initiative. Kaye and Resnick (1994) suggest attending to what they call the six Rs of participation: recognition, respect, role, relationship, reward, and results. To get started, consider sharing the following recruitment invitation messages, which reflect the six Rs of participation and recommendations from the authors of the *Collaboration Toolkit* (Rinehart, Laszlo, & Briscoe, 2001):

Recognition and respect: Team members will gain system-wide recognition and respect.

Role: You can fulfill your professional leadership obligation to contribute to our profession.

Relationship: You will enjoy learning with others who are committed to changing their instruction.

Reward: This is an amazing opportunity to learn new skills and improve your practice.

Results: Imagine the sense of accomplishment you will feel from making a difference in learner outcomes!

These messages are designed to recruit interest and invite educators to investigate UDL as a member of your collaborative team. Maybe these ideas aren't a comfortable fit for you and you want to try something different. Go for it! Whatever approach you use to create your collaborative team, remember that inspiration is a better recruitment tool than coercion.

> *If you want to build a ship,*
> *don't drum up people to collect wood and don't assign them tasks and work,*
> *but rather teach them to long for the endless immensity of the sea.*
>
> —ANTOINE DE SAINT-EXUPÉRY, author of *The Little Prince*

As your project proceeds, you can increase interest by promoting your shared vision and the authentic achievements of your action plan. In short, you'll find that your team's success becomes an invitation to new members to join and current members to persist. For instance, reflecting on 15 years of building collaborative efforts within the US centered on improving services for students with disabilities, leaders of the IDEA Partnership concluded that the fuel for attracting new team members and keeping original members involved was the actual experience of ongoing engagement and actionable learning (Cashman, Linehan, & Rosser, 2007). In other words, *experiencing continuous improvement and real results* encouraged coalition members to sustain their active participation.

WATCH FOR UDL

Engagement

- Recruit interest.
- Sustain effort and persistence.
- Provide options for self-reflection.

Billy Burke of BCPS shared a dynamic example (Burke, 2017). He discovered that working on a successful collaborative team was energizing for veteran educators and enriching for those new to the profession. In fact, many who at first expressed reluctance had the opportunity to work on effective collaborative teams and now proclaim it is the best professional development they've ever had. They expanded their knowledge of learners' needs and mastered new instructional practices that they were able to use over and over again for years.

Goal Directed, Interdependent, and Mutually Accountable

As mentioned earlier, your UDL initiative needs to be *goal directed*. Successful collaborative teams share a mutually desirable vision or goal that is beyond the scope of any one individual's knowledge and skills. If you have questions about the importance of developing a clear, shared vision, you may want to review Chapter 3.

Hackman (2002) argues that without a shared goal, a team is actually *not* a team, but rather a *co-acting group*. The key difference is that the work of co-acting groups is not interdependent. For example, insurance adjusters in the same office may all do the same type of tasks, but typically they are not dependent on each other's performance. On the other hand, an orchestra is a highly *interdependent* team because individual members need to play together to create a successful musical performance. In like manner, educators involved in your UDL implementation project will depend on and draw from each other's diverse expertise and accomplish their shared goal as an interdependent team.

Adding to the concept of interdependency, DuFour, DuFour, Eaker, & Many (2006) describe collaborative teams as *mutually accountable*, illustrated by the following sports analogy:

- In golf, a foursome plays together, but they approach the final tee as independent golfers, each with individual scores. Mutual accountability is not present.

- In basketball, each team member makes individual points, but they are all accountable for the team's performance because the team accrues one score for their joint efforts on the court during the game. In this case, the team is mutually accountable.

Your UDL implementation team members should hold each other accountable for accomplishing their shared goal in a comparable manner. Each team member should definitely have personal goals they want to achieve, but *mutual accountability* toward your shared vision should be your team's prime focal point.

Shared Responsibility and Resources

Through their pioneering work on coteaching, Friend and Cook (1992) augmented the notion of effective team collaboration with these specific components:

- Collaboration is based on *parity* among partners.

- Interactions are rooted in *shared responsibility* for planning, problem-solving, and decision-making.

- Team members share resources.

Like other descriptions of collaboration, Friend and Cook emphasize that all team members need to attend to a *common goal* and that their work should be grounded by *shared accountability* for outcomes. Of course, all collaborations, including coteaching and collaborative relationships, are shaped by the personalities and working styles of the teachers involved (Rao and Berquist, 2017). You'll find that applying the UDL guidelines to your decision-making process provides a shared construct, a common language, and an approach for collaboration that ensures that educators focus on ways to design and deliver flexible, engaging, and inclusive lessons for all the students in their inclusive environments.

Before we move on, let's take a moment to clarify the difference between cooperation and collaboration. Even though collaboration is associated with common cooperative behaviors and working styles, the two characteristics are not the same. What's the difference? *Cooperation,* such as communicating and sharing information and coordinating access to resources, is something an individual does as she participates in a group. Cooperation facilitates participation. Yet, one person's cooperation does not typically determine the learning of the entire group. In contrast, *collaboration* presumes that all members of the group not only communicate and share with each other, but that they create or produce something together. Because a collaborative group is interdependent and mutually accountable, the learning of all the members of the group depends on the contributions and collaboration of each individual member. (Nussbaum-Beach & Ritter Hall, 2012).

REFLECTION How collaborative is your learning environment?

MAKE IT ACTIONABLE To assume that collaboration exists is problematic, and to estimate its impact on your UDL implementation action plan without evidence is a mistake. Therefore, collaboration should be evaluated regularly. A variety of tools are available to evaluate collaborative characteristics of teams. Solution Tree offers many free tools and resources including measures of collaboration on its website, *https://www.solutiontree.com/free-resources*. Bright Morning, an organization established by coaching expert Elena Aguilar, also makes several team collaboration tools available on its website, *http://brightmorningteam.com/*. To measure collaborative participation based on the six Rs of participation, check out an evaluation tool developed by Wolff (2002) available from *https://www.tomwolff.com/resources/backer.pdf*.

RECOGNITION Develop educators' expertise for applying UDL to their practice by providing customized professional learning opportunities, including professional development workshops, professional learning communities (PLCs), and coaching.

UDL Professional Development

You are always providing professional development (PD) in a learning organization. Since the beginning of your UDL implementation project—as you've progressed through the Explore and Prepare phases—you've been building an understanding of the UDL framework through PD. The key difference in what you did during previous phases and what you do during the Integrate phase is that you move beyond describing the "what" of UDL to teaching the "how." Although you may still include concepts underlying the UDL framework during the Integrate phase, the primary purpose of PD at this point is to develop educators' expertise for applying UDL to their practice.

WHISTLE-STOP During the Explore phase, you built awareness of UDL by introducing the UDL framework to your UDL implementation team and others in decision-making roles. If you haven't accomplished this step, see Chapter 4 for an overview of the concepts you should share. During the Prepare phase, you established a UDL climate of high expectations, acceptance, and respect for learner variability by offering educators an opportunity to examine their beliefs about learners and instruction and clarifying the notions that undergird the UDL framework. If you haven't yet provided PD aimed at these topics, review Chapter 5.

Burke (2017) discusses the fundamental impact on teaching and learning that resulted when the Baltimore County Public Schools in Maryland adopted UDL. He states that after years of traditional PD on UDL the "real shift toward UDL integration" occurred when PD began to focus on

> . . . *job-embedded learning, with coaches providing support around resources and application. Teachers worked to design instruction using the UDL principles and formed a professional learning community (PLC) that met monthly to share resources and ideas, triumphs, and barriers—and to celebrate successes. (p.169)*

To maximize the power of professional learning on UDL, Burke emphasizes that PD providers need to model the UDL framework, address learner variability among their adult learners, and offer the opportunity to participants to actually experience UDL as a learner.

> *The power of professional learning is maximized when the instructional activities model effective teaching practices.*
>
> —BILLY BURKE, Chief of Organizational Effectiveness, Baltimore County Public Schools

Create Your UDL Professional Development Plan

One of the primary tasks to accomplish during the Integrate phase is to develop and implement a PD plan focused on providing educators with the beliefs, knowledge, and practices they need to apply UDL to instruction. Your UDL PD plan should not be developed in isolation. Consult applicable educator professional standards, certification, and licensing requirements and existing teacher and/or employee evaluation processes to identify relevant alignments. In this way, you can provide incentives for your UDL team members to participate in your UDL PD plan offerings. Other components you should address include securing PD funding, allocating meeting space, scheduling within the timeline of your project, and avoiding conflicts with other PD activities (particularly any mandatory PD that educators are required to attend). If possible, you should also provide documentation or evidence of PD participation that team members can use for maintaining or advancing their professional status, certification, or licenses.

Assess Needs and Define Personal Learning Goals

Anne Beninghof (2014), a seasoned presenter and internationally recognized consultant, calls for thoughtful PD design in her book *Caffeinated Learning: How to Design and Conduct Rich, Robust Professional Training*. Most importantly, she reminds us that planning PD for adult learners starts with assessing participants' needs. Begin by surveying your educators' PD interests with targeted questions, or ask them to complete a needs assessment. The goals and objectives of your UDL PD plan can then zero in on relevant areas of interest and needs. To enhance authenticity, offer educators who attend your PD sessions the opportunity to define their personal learning goals at the beginning of every session and to reflect on whether they achieved them at the end of each session.

What Comes First?

In a critique of conventional PD, Guskey (2000) asked a provocative "chicken vs. egg" question: "Do educators alter their beliefs and then change their practice or is it the other way around?" How would you respond to this question? Since your perspective might influence the goals of your PD programs, let's explore this concept further. According to Guskey, PD programs typically target three goals in the following order: first to affect educators' attitudes and beliefs, second to improve instructional practices, and finally to impact learner outcomes. Contrary to what some believe, research shows that educators' attitudes and beliefs actually change in response to seeing differences in learner performance. PD that only addresses educators' attitudes and beliefs will not lead to sustainable transformation. Therefore, effective PD should address all three goals simultaneously rather than individually or sequentially over time. To successfully change practice, every UDL PD session should

- advance beliefs about learners and instruction,
- clarify UDL theory, and
- provide specific UDL strategies that can be immediately applied in the learning environment.

Effective Professional Development

Education researchers have investigated the effectiveness of professional development and uncovered common elements that impact student outcomes. For example, Darling-Hammond, Hyler, and Gardener (2017) identified the following seven elements of effective PD:

1. Focuses on content
2. Incorporates active learning
3. Supports collaboration
4. Uses models of effective practice

5. Provides coaching and expert support

6. Offers feedback and reflection

7. Is of sustained duration

You can use this list to incorporate best practices as you design your UDL professional development plan.

UDL Professional Learning Communities

In agreement with Guskey's PD goals, a key strategy for developing educator expertise during the Integrate phase is creating professional learning communities (PLCs). PLCs are defined as "a collective of educators who always strive to perform at the ultimate potential, working together to learn, grow, and improve the professional practice of teaching in order to maximize student learning" (Hall & Simeral, 2008, p. 17). PLCs are recognized as a powerful staff development approach and a potent strategy for school change and improvement (Darling-Hammond, et al., 2017; Hord, 1997). The goal of PLCs is to jointly enhance the professional effectiveness of educators so that learners benefit.

Berquist (2017) highlights the difference between so-called "traditional one-shot" PD and high-quality, ongoing professional learning provided through PLCs. The former typically places educators in passive roles as they attend individual workshops about instructional techniques or curriculum strategies and receive limited or no classroom application. In contrast, PLCs provide "contextually supportive and collaborative" opportunities to simultaneously reconsider beliefs, construct new knowledge, and learn innovative skills through inquiry-based collaborative experiences (Berquist, 2017, p. 27).

There may be PLCs within your system now. Some may be organized by curriculum or subject areas and others may be organized by learner groupings or grade levels. Because UDL applies to all learning and all age levels, UDL-PLCs often cross grade and subject areas. Be mindful that grade-level team or department meetings, faculty meetings, data presentations, curriculum writing, assessment scoring, or lesson planning may be *mislabeled as PLCs*. Inserting these functions into your UDL-PLC can undermine its purpose and erode its effectiveness. *Stay true to the goal of your UDL-PLC.*

UDL-PLCs can be facilitated by an identified member of the group or the leadership role can rotate or be shared by various members. UDL-PLCs can also be facilitated by an outside consultant, skilled facilitator, or instructional leader. Whichever leadership model you choose, it should be one that your team decides will work for them and maintain its authenticity. To determine if your UDL-PLC is authentic, ask these questions:

- Do members of your UDL-PLC design the content and processes of their meetings to advance their professional learning?

- Do the UDL-PLC members take collective responsibility for the goals of the group?

- Do leaders misappropriate time for agenda items not related to the UDL-PLC goals?

- Do your UDL-PLC members focus on developing supportive and shared leadership that invites shared decision-making?

Infuse UDL into Your PLCs

The chief characteristic of UDL-PLCs is that they focus on learning how to apply the UDL principles to enhance instruction. Typically, UDL-PLCs learn together, over time, through a combination of these three models:

Book study: Educators jointly read and discuss texts and articles that explore UDL theory or application. Some recommended books include

- *Universal Design for Learning: Theory and Practice* (2014) by Meyer et al.

- *Design and Deliver: Planning and Teaching using Universal Design for Learning* (2014) by Nelson

Lesson study: Educators jointly learn about and explore strategies for applying UDL to their lesson planning. Some recommended resources include

- *Your UDL Lesson Planner: The Step-by-Step Guide to Teaching All Learners* (2016) by Ralabate

- *Culturally Responsive Design for English Learners: The UDL Approach* (2017) by Ralabate and Nelson

Inquiry-based problem solving: Educators use an inquiry process to collaboratively employ UDL to address instructional problems of practice in their classrooms. Some recommended resources include

- *UDL Now! A Teacher's Guide to Applying Universal Design for Learning in the Classroom* (2016) by Novak
- *Crosswalk between Universal Design for Learning and the Danielson Framework for Teaching* (2012) by CAST & the Danielson Framework
- *Instructional Rounds in Education: A Network Approach to Improving Learning and Teaching* (2009) by City, Elmore, Fiarman, & Teitel

Keeping in mind that flexibility and learner variability should guide your approach, the following UDL-PLC inquiry process may assist you to get started. It outlines a six-step continuous improvement cycle:

1. Set learning goals that are based on high expectations for all learners and that are aligned with appropriate standards.
2. Design learning environments and lessons that consider the principles of UDL and systematic learner variability in the selection, creation, and use of instruction, curriculum, and physical space.
3. Define progress monitoring techniques or an assessment plan that emphasizes regular formative assessment to evaluate student progress and performance consistent with the UDL principles.
4. Select instructional strategies, techniques, or methods that align with culturally responsive pedagogy and are consistent with the principles of UDL.
5. Select relevant curricular materials, tools, and technologies that support learning, add value, and provide accessible, flexible, learning environments for learners.
6. Use student/learner data to reflect on, refine, and enhance practice with PLC colleagues in a vibrant learning community. (Based on Dufour et al., 2006; Ralabate, 2016, and Thessin & Starr, 2011)

UDL-PLCs should meet regularly—at least monthly. And it may work best for your PLC members to meet during the work day (e.g., during planning periods) rather than before or after work. Online sessions may be preferred to on-site meetings. César E. Chávez High School in Houston, Texas, where the authors have consulted, offers an illustration of the types of options you can consider:

- UDL-PLCs meet during the day in lieu of individual planning periods or department meetings.

- Full-day Saturday sessions are scheduled at set times during the year.

- Brief after-school sessions are held periodically to allow for cross-PLC sharing and opportunities for facilitated group decision-making.

- Substitutes are provided to cover classes several times a year so that UDL-PLC members can observe each other's UDL implementation strategies in prescheduled walkthroughs.

UDL Coaching

Instead of group UDL-PLC sessions or in conjunction with them, some UDL implementation projects construct facilitated learning sessions between UDL coaches and individual educators. For example, Bartholomew Consolidated School Corporation (BCSC) in Columbus, Indiana, established a district-wide UDL coordinator and building-level Instructional Consultation Team facilitators who offered individual sessions to support UDL instructional practices (Center on Technology and Disability, n.d.). Similarly, Wisconsin's OASD (discussed in Chapter 5) realized the powerful role of the instructional coach and created positions in each building for UDL coaches.

Coaching should be skill-based and personalized. Berquist (2017) argues that UDL coaching sessions should provide educators with opportunities to articulate, compare, contrast, and evaluate their beliefs about teaching and learning. Over time, carefully constructed coaching sessions help educators confront their existing conceptions about instruction as they integrate new practices. Coaching sessions often use a lesson-planning or constructive problem-solving approach and offer ample opportunities for self-reflection. Coaches may model lessons, observe and critique lessons, and offer resources. Both online and on-site coaching can be successful, although on-site offers the additional opportunity to observe instruction and changes in practice in real-time.

Developing a trust relationship is critical to the coach-educator relationship. That's why coaches are typically peers of equal rank or independent consultants rather than supervisors. Frankly, the power imbalance between educators and administrators who have evaluation duties complicates the coach-educator relationship.

> **MAKE IT ACTIONABLE** You might remember the UDL Professional Development Needs Assessment survey that was described in Chapter 5 (available in the "Resources" section). Originally developed by Bartholomew Consolidated School Corporation (BCSC), a public school district in Columbus, Indiana, it was adapted by CAST during the Gates-funded UDL Implementation Project. The PD needs assessment survey results will help guide your professional development decision-making.

> **ACTION AND EXPRESSION** Evaluate the efficacy of established policies, processes, and procedures, infuse UDL as needed, and create new practices that align with the UDL framework.

Alignment with UDL

To facilitate smooth integration of UDL, you'll need to critically evaluate the efficacy of the implementation infrastructure within your current system. What are the current priorities? Are they supportive or will they be significant barriers to effective UDL implementation? Unless your system is unusual, changes will be necessary. But if you start with leveraging what already exists and infuse the UDL framework, you can be less disruptive and ultimately more successful.

The Four Ps: Policies, Processes, Procedures, and Practices

In any system—whether it's a national or regional education system; a state, province, district, or college; or a department or school—a myriad of structures, rules, and ways of doing things can impact your UDL implementation project. This complex, interconnected, multilayered maze forms your system's implementation infrastructure.

Some elements are helpful, and others are barriers to effective implementation. You can't and shouldn't try to change everything at once. But, where do you start? Look first at what we call *The Four Ps: Policies, processes, procedures, and practices.*

Policies

Education policies are the principles, laws, and rules that govern the operation of the education enterprise, i.e., your system. Based on the underlying philosophy of the leaders and community, policy sets direction and can be used to guide decision-making. For example, national policies that govern K–12 public education in the US include federal laws, such as the Elementary and Secondary Education Act (ESEA) and the Individuals with Disabilities Education Act (IDEA). The Higher Education Act (HEA) sets policies for how US postsecondary education is implemented. Although known by a variety of names, policy-setting bodies at the regional, state, provincial, local, and district level include the state board of education, department of public instruction, local board of education, and in some cases, the school council, governing committee, or trustees. These rule-making bodies establish the philosophy, goals, and guiding principles for how your system operates. Most federal or state policies identify and fund required programs and staff positions. Individual education leaders also interpret and determine policies. For instance, principals define expectations for educators and learners and department chairs and curriculum supervisors establish timelines for delivery of instruction and funding for resources.

Processes

A *process* is a systematic set of actions to achieve a specific goal. It defines the big picture or breadth of things that must be completed and highlights the key work elements you must accomplish. Processes are often required by established policies. For example, to safeguard the civil rights of students with disabilities, schools are required to provide a set of notifications and complaint opportunities to parents under the IDEA's due process provisions (Turnbull, Stowe, & Huerta, 2007). A familiar process defined by national and state policies, Response to Intervention (RTI), also known as Multitiered Systems of Support (MTSS), involves a series of steps educators take in response to students' needs. The RTI approach begins with high-quality, inclusive core instruction for all learners (i.e., Tier 1) and continues as needed with levels of instruction intensity or interventions (i.e., Tier 2 and Tier 3) (RTI Action Network, n.d.). Teacher evaluation is another example of a process.

Procedures

Although processes encompass the breadth of actions, procedures detail the depth of specific methods or official steps you perform. Sometimes procedures are referred to as protocols. For instance, standardized assessments and progress monitoring procedures may be considered protocols because they must be conducted in a precise manner to give valid results. Behavior intervention procedures are another example of protocols because they often include exact responses to student behavior that educators must follow.

Practices

Practices involve repeated activities, usually in an effort to improve your skills. For example, a musician practices her instrument and a golfer practices his swing. Practices also refer to the teaching strategies you use to apply UDL to your instruction. Some lesson-planning formats demand specific instructional practices, such as visible learning goals, posted anchor charts, using call and response routines, starting with an anticipatory set or providing guiding questions.

Integrate with What Exists

Before you develop a list of new structures to adopt, your UDL implementation team should systematically review the policies, processes, procedures, and practices that currently exist to determine if they can be leveraged to support UDL implementation.

These examples can serve as models:

Indiana's Bartholomew Consolidated School Corporation (BCSC). One of the first accomplishments of BCSC, an Indiana public school system, was adjusting district *policies* to align with the UDL framework. They looked at their district's philosophy, core values, and beliefs and identified how those elements aligned with the UDL principles and guidelines. They then adopted the UDL framework as an overarching or umbrella framework for the district so that all learning environments, instructional programs, and practices are infused with notions associated with UDL, such as learner variability, flexibility, accessibility, collaboration, and life-long learning (BCSC, 2009).

Wisconsin's Oconomowoc Area School District (OASD). As OASD began to integrate UDL within their system, they engaged in a research-mapping process to determine which system policies, processes, procedures, and practices already existed that would support UDL implementation and which needed to change to move UDL forward. For example, as mentioned earlier, they quickly realized the importance of developing a position dedicated to UDL implementation and coaching. To make this happen, district leaders used existing resources by repurposing funds from both special education and curriculum and instruction programs (funded by federal and state policies). OASD also recognized that the traditional school librarian position (delineated by the Board of Education and funded by local funds) could be reimagined to align to the future-ready framework that focuses on instructional coaching. This adjustment placed additional educators in classrooms as coaches.

In addition, OASD reconfigured their process for curriculum adoption to ensure infusion of the UDL framework. They now have a team of teachers who analyze all curriculum and textbook adoptions with a rubric aligned to the UDL framework. Recognizing that their professional learning needed to include experts in UDL implementation, they've offered an intensive summer institute for the past three years that brings experts in from across the US to support professional learning communities dedicated to infusing UDL into teaching practices. The district team truly believes that their integrated comprehensive service model that relies on learning specialists who work with all students and teachers to identify proactive instruction rather than special educators who work with only a few students and teachers is crucial for UDL implementation. They continually work to shift district policies, processes, procedures, and practices to ensure that they are moving from preparation to integration.

WHAT DO WE DO NOW?

Steps you might consider doing now should focus on ways to foster collaboration and develop educator expertise. This is an appropriate time to evaluate current policies, processes, procedures, and practices used in your system. Spotlights 6.1, 6.2, and 6.3 will guide your efforts.

Foster Collaboration

The first task you may want to undertake is evaluating the level of collaborative relationships that are currently supported within your system. Because none of the available evaluation tools assess elements of UDL, such as flexibility and choice, you may want to use Spotlight 6.1, which is a survey that provides a means of analyzing the collaborative features experienced by your UDL implementation team. If preferred, responses can be anonymous. Even though it is not standardized, you can use this tool to gauge relative changes in how participants view collaboration within your UDL project by administering it periodically and monitoring trends in reported perspectives.

Develop Educator Expertise

Based on data you already possess or on an interview process or survey that you employ, determine what educators already believe and know about learners and instruction. Use this information to develop your UDL PD plan.

As you develop your PD plan for your UDL implementation initiative, you may find it helpful to review the list of recommended characteristics of effective PD that are outlined in Spotlight 6.2. Note that these characteristics align with adult learning theory as well as UDL.

Evaluate, Infuse, and Create

Your UDL implementation team should conduct a review of your system's implementation infrastructure—The Four Ps: policies, processes, procedures, and practices—that will impact your UDL implementation efforts. Using a collaborative inquiry approach, your team should

- identify what exists,
- evaluate whether it is a potential barrier that will hinder or a support that will enhance your efforts,
- determine what gaps are present that need to be filled, and
- create new structures, as needed, to fill your identified gaps.

Prioritize which items need to change immediately and which can wait. Remember to use authentic data or evidence for your decisions and to infuse the UDL framework throughout your work. You may find that using Spotlight 6.3 can jumpstart your implementation infrastructure review.

SPOTLIGHT 6.1:
Gauging Collaboration

Directions

This survey should be completed by everyone. Results should be compiled, graphed, shared, and discussed by your team.

REFLECTION	N/A (0)	STRONGLY DISAGREE (1)	SOMEWHAT DISAGREE (2)	SOMEWHAT AGREE (3)	STRONGLY AGREE (4)
Our shared vision aligns with my beliefs about learners and instruction.					
We support high expectations of all learners with engaging, authentic instruction.					
Our meetings are efficient, purposeful, and allow for a meaningful exchange of ideas.					
I'm not comfortable when others observe me teaching.					
I have time to examine learner performance with my team/colleagues.					

REFLECTION	N/A (0)	STRONGLY DISAGREE (1)	SOMEWHAT DISAGREE (2)	SOMEWHAT AGREE (3)	STRONGLY AGREE (4)
We regularly provide each other with mastery-oriented feedback focused on improving practice.					
We are respected and recognized for our contributions and expertise.					
I feel I have little choice, flexibility, and/or impact on decisions related to my instruction.					
Regular reflection on data—what worked, and what didn't work in my lessons—results in valuable ideas and suggestions.					
Collaboration has helped me improve application of UDL in my practice.					

SPOTLIGHT 6.2:
Evaluating UDL Professional Development

Directions

Reflect on the following characteristics as you develop your plans for professional development.

CHARACTERISTICS	STRONGLY AGREE (4)	AGREE (3)	DISAGREE (2)	STRONGLY DISAGREE (1)	NOT ADDRESSED (0)
PD is aligned with UDL theory.					
PD is aligned with adult learning theory.					
PD respects learner variability and allows for choice and flexibility.					
PD addresses content knowledge and instructional practices that will improve student outcomes.					
PD is relevant and built on educators' practices and beliefs.					
PD encourages high levels of engagement.					

CHARACTERISTICS	STRONGLY AGREE (4)	AGREE (3)	DISAGREE (2)	STRONGLY DISAGREE (1)	NOT ADDRESSED (0)
PD highlights critical features and provides strategies in a coherent and focused manner (i.e., not fragmented).					
PD provides for intensive, authentic follow-up including support in teachers' classrooms.					
PD is actively supported by the administration/management.					
PD is site-based, job embedded, and offers long term support.					

Based on Waldron & McLeskey (2010) and Berquist (2017)

SPOTLIGHT 6.3:
Evaluating the Four Ps

Directions

1. Ask your UDL implementation team members to think about the policies, processes, procedures, and practices that currently exist within your system.

2. Ask them to capture one item each on Post-its.

3. Ask them to add their set of Post-its to a wall or board that can be accessed and seen by all team members.

4. Ask a subgroup to reorganize the items by category—policy, process, procedure, practice. Keep duplicates together. Categorizing clarifies responsibility and ways to make changes. Consult with the original authors if the subgroup is unfamiliar with the item.

5. Jointly complete the following table. As you do, ask these questions:

    a. How does this item contribute to our ability to engage learners, flexibly represent information and build comprehension, or offer choice and support expression and development of executive functions?

    b. To what extent can we strengthen this item by infusing the UDL framework?

    c. If it is a barrier, how can we reduce its influence? Should we eliminate it?

    d. What authentic evidence confirms our decision?

6. To increase efficiency, you may divide into subgroups of two to three members, each assigned to a different category.

7. Review the completed evaluation with the full team. Use consensus to develop agreement and rank the items in terms of priority for change. Solicit volunteers or assign responsibility to specific team member(s) for any changes that you decide to pursue.

ITEM	CATEGORY (POLICY, PROCESS, PROCEDURE, OR PRACTICE)	BARRIER OR SUPPORT?	EVIDENCE	STRENGTHEN OR ELIMINATE?	PRIORITY FOR CHANGE #
Example: MTSS	**Example:** Process—Local process based on state policy	**Example:** Support—Encourages high expectations in general ed (Tier 1)	**Example:** Student test results show improved performance in general ed	**Example:** Add UDL as umbrella for instruction of all learners	**Example:** #1—Principal to recommend new language to MTSS description
Example: Required unit exams	**Example:** Procedure—Departmental assessment procedure	**Example:** Barrier—Limits choice of expression and performance	**Example:** Unit exams are the only ongoing assessment used at this time	**Example:** Eliminate requirement to provide time for more formative assessments	**Example:** #3—Department chairs to amend assessment procedures
Example: Textbook adoption	**Example:** Process—Based solely on administrator recommendations	**Example:** Barrier—Limits learner accessibility and flexibility	**Example:** Required texts do not include learner options for engagement, recognition and action and expression	**Example:** Add teacher review committee	**Example:** #2—Textbook adoption process to be amended to add teacher review

ESSENTIAL QUESTIONS

1. How collaborative is your system?

2. What do educators need to know about UDL practices to apply the UDL principles to their instruction and decision-making?

3. How can PLCs and coaching effectively enhance UDL implementation in your system?

4. To what extent will incentives, such as focused planning time, stipends, or PD credits encourage infusion of the UDL framework within your system?

5. In what ways do existing local/state/regional/national initiatives and requirements align with UDL?

6. How can your policies, processes, procedures, and practices support and sustain UDL implementation?

WHAT'S NEXT? Chapter 7 discusses how to scale your UDL implementation efforts.

7

Scale

GUIDING QUESTIONS

- How do we create and support a collaborative community of practice?

- In what ways can we expand our UDL implementation practices across our learning environment or system?

- What policies, procedures, processes, and structures are most effective for growing UDL implementation?

LET'S HEAR FROM KATHY, A PROFESSIONAL LEARNING TEACHER IN THE BALTIMORE COUNTY PUBLIC SCHOOLS (BCPS).

As you read in Chapter 6, Baltimore County Public Schools (BCPS), in Maryland, use UDL as a framework to reimagine the design of professional learning and empower adult learners to make decisions. Throughout this chapter, you will hear from Kathy Kelbaugh, a professional learning teacher in BCPS, about how she and her colleagues have worked to scale UDL across a feeder pattern including five elementary schools, a middle school, and a high school in the same community.

Kathy offers this description of their work:

At Prettyboy Elementary, we first worked to scale UDL by building opportunities for our teachers to connect with other teachers in our feeder pattern, initially by engaging in a UDL Now! [Novak, 2016] book study and then by organizing learning walks across schools. Small groups of teachers began to connect with one another around their shared interest in UDL. We had pockets of UDL implementation occurring with great success in some of our classrooms where we had spent a significant amount of time focusing on shifting our instruction to be more learner centered. Moving these successes to additional classrooms, and even schools, in our feeder required a more thoughtful approach and additional support for our adult learners. We are fortunate in BCPS to have one professional learning teacher assigned to each school. While debriefing at a vertical team meeting, the professional learning teachers in our feeder pattern recognized that there were similarities in the needs of the teachers in their buildings and we realized that there was great power in collaborating to design professional learning opportunities that would be offered to any teacher in our feeder pattern (K. Kelbaugh, personal interview, September 2018).

After the initial decision to expand positive practices across the seven schools in the feeder pattern, the professional learning teachers decided that they needed a structure to make this work happen efficiently. In BCPS, teachers can earn continuing professional development credit by participating in professional learning. The team designed and delivered a series of professional development experiences that could be mixed and matched to earn 1, 2, or 3 credits. Sessions were delivered by the professional learning teachers and were open to any teacher in the feeder pattern, regardless of which school hosted the session. Learning walks were also offered monthly, giving teachers of different age groups, levels, and content areas a glimpse into what UDL practices look like across settings. These opportunities promoted the growth of a community of practice and support shared learning across the feeder pattern. The following list describes some of the options included in the feeder-pattern professional learning model that help to scale UDL practices using the existing professional learning processes.

- Conduct needs assessment to determine areas of interest for teachers.
- Structure the learning experience to allow for choice.

- Provide opportunities to access professional development in different ways (on-site, online, in home school, school-school visits).

- Offer on-site (i.e., face-to-face), digital, and blended options.

- Harness the power of technology to organize materials (first through OneNote and then through Schoology).

- Develop a digital newsletter to keep all participants informed and connected.

- Ensure that each session leader provides feedback to participants after each session.

- Provide time for reflection after each session (collected on a universal reflection tool).

- Offer learning walks to observe application of new learning.

- Support collaboration and community by organizing job-alike planning sessions.

- Spotlight experts in the feeder pattern and encourage them to offer sessions on relevant topics.

- Use social media to connect across schools.

SCALE

Emphasis during the Scale phase is on *growing* your UDL implementation project by expanding and extending the collaborative environment and successful structures and practices established during the Integrate phase. Pathways during the Scale phase include

- *promoting a UDL community of practice* to support shared collaborative learning across your system,

- *expanding practices* to create an integrated, system-wide approach to instruction and decision-making, and

- *enhancing effective implementation* through policies, processes, procedures, and organizational structures infused with the UDL principles.

ENGAGEMENT Promote a UDL community of practice to support shared learning across your system.

Collaborative Community

As your UDL implementation project begins to grow, there is an additional level of complexity in collaboration that includes establishing a community of practice (CoP) focused on UDL. In 1991, Lave and Wenger coined the term *community of practice* to describe a group of people who share a common interest or concern and engage in *collective learning* that results in practices and social relationships that sustain the group's work.

Promote a Collaborative UDL Community of Practice

Why would you want to build a UDL community of practice (UDL-CoP) if you've already created a collaborative team? To answer this question, let's look at the underlying rationale for forming your UDL team. Any team is defined by its agreed-upon task and its cohesiveness is linked to work completion. Once the team's task is finished, it can disband. As it accomplishes its identified goals, a collaborative team can begin to lose momentum over time. Most of us have seen this happen. In contrast, a CoP forms to address a *shared learning need* and is held together by the relationships that develop among its members. CoPs are *relationship-driven* because their members derive value from learning together (Team BE, 2011). Since your UDL initiative is targeting long-standing transformative changes, your educators need to have a sense of momentum that is supported by a stronger bond than merely accomplishing tasks. To create transformative change, you'll want your collaborative team to grow into a UDL-CoP.

According to Cambridge, Kaplan, and Suter (2005), pertinent activities related to creating sustainable CoPs include

- *building relationships* of trust, mutual respect, reciprocity, and commitment;
- learning and developing *shared practice* based on existing knowledge;
- generating and discovering *new knowledge;* and
- taking purposeful action to produce *shared resources.*

As members of your CoP interact, they generate commitment to each other and your community's shared vision and identity. They form dynamic, long-lasting relationships and create practices that, in turn, strengthen the group's capacity to learn and work together. The continuously improving, self-sustaining, cyclical nature of an effective UDL-CoP is fundamental to transforming instruction.

> *It takes collaboration across a community to develop better skills for better lives.*
>
> —JOSE ANGEL GURRIA, economist

What's the Difference Between UDL-PLCs and UDL-CoPs?

A professional learning community (PLC) is one type of community of practice. As discussed in Chapter 6, your UDL-PLC specifically addresses professional practice. It provides educators in your system with effective professional development and offers them the opportunity to refine their own instructional skills as they benefit from and add to the expertise of their PLC colleagues. The key difference between PLCs and CoPs is related to their membership. Members of PLCs are classroom educators or instructional staff who directly work with learners. On the other hand, the membership of CoPs is purposefully broad. In addition to instructional staff, CoPs often include administrators, supervisors, other educational leaders, ancillary staff, community members, and others in decision-making roles. Administrators and supervisors who are members of your UDL-CoP take on a supportive role rather than direct instruction of learners. As a result, your UDL-CoP is uniquely able to apply the UDL framework to decision-making and developing systemic organizational structures.

Berquist (2017) describes "leadership PLCs" that are essentially UDL-CoPs. They are committed to UDL and their overarching goals focus on collective learning. Specifically, members want to strengthen, refine, and expand each other's practice, enrich the learning environment, and improve learner outcomes. UDL-CoPs differ from other administrative or management teams. First, instead of defining unique areas of responsibility for each leader, all members of the UDL-CoP—administrators as well as classroom teachers—share responsibilities for addressing any barriers that might exist. Second, they mutually determine the content and processes that will lead to their system's continuous improvement. And lastly, they celebrate and take joint ownership of their successes. Administrators or supervisors who are not CoP members may sometimes participate in meetings, but they do not take the lead. Likewise, outside facilitators offer processes and protocols to enhance collaborative decision-making but do not assume responsibility for setting the agenda or making decisions for the group. Berquist (2017) aptly describes the role of facilitators as serving as the "guide on the side" instead of the "sage on the stage." They remain mindful that UDL-CoP members need to exercise shared authority over their own learning.

Establish Your UDL-CoP

Let's explore actions specifically associated with establishing your UDL-CoP. After your first set of volunteers commit to your UDL initiative, preliminary details that must be tackled are

- defining communication protocols,
- developing collaborative learning goals,
- establishing knowledge sharing procedures, and
- determining roles, leadership structures, and meeting times.

Keep in mind that although these tasks seem mundane, fostering a collaborative, sustainable, sense of community begins with building mutual commitment and understanding through shared decision-making, even at this initial stage. You may be tempted to just get started and try to make all of these decisions by yourself. If you do, you will deny your CoP members a vital opportunity to establish relationships and to learn how to productively work together.

> **WHISTLE-STOP** If you'd like to do a deep dive on communities of practice, read Wenger's work, *Communities of Practice: Learning, Meaning, and Identity* (1998) and the IDEA Partnership's *Communities of Practice: A New Approach to Solving Complex Educational Problems* (2007).

Berquist (2017) suggests the following considerations for designing your UDL-CoP:

- Conduct an initial needs assessment to determine agenda topics.
- After your initial meeting, use regular formative assessments to determine continuing needs and interests.
- Ensure that meetings are held on-site to allow access to instructional settings.
- Manage logistics, cofacilitate, or share leadership with practitioner UDL-PLCs and on-site administrators who may or may not be members of your UDL-CoP.
- Ground meeting agenda in authentic practice by sharing problems of practice and participating in learning walks through classrooms or learning environments.
- Embed capacity building skills focused on community learning.
- Use collaborative structures for meetings, such as establishing group norms or expectations, jointly creating agenda, and utilizing shared decision-making protocols.
- Share feedback and follow-up steps after the meeting.

A distinctive attribute of a UDL-CoP is that the UDL principles are consciously applied to its interactions, products, and processes. Consequently, their members hold high expectations about respecting variability and offering accessibility, flexibility, choice, and supports that promote meaningful experiences.

WATCH FOR UDL

Selected Engagement Guidelines

- Provide options for recruiting interest.
    - Optimize individual choice and autonomy.
    - Optimize relevance, value, and authenticity.
- Provide options for sustaining effort and persistence.
    - Heighten salience of goals and objectives.
    - Vary demands and resources to optimize challenge.
- Provide options for self-regulation.
    - Promote expectations and beliefs that optimize motivation.
    - Develop self-assessment and reflection.

© CAST, 2014. Used with permission.

Although your UDL-CoP will define customized, shared learning goals, its main purposes always must include these two crucial tasks:

- Creating new knowledge about UDL implementation
- Sharing best practices aligned with UDL

As discussed in the last chapter, don't allow other discussion items to divert your attention from your shared goals or otherwise erode your focus from UDL implementation.

MAKE IT ACTIONABLE Determine if your team is defined solely by task completion or if it is undergirded by the value that members derive from working together. Is your team relationship-driven? Is it a UDL-CoP? To delve deeper into how to apply UDL while establishing a sustainable, collaborative CoP, review Table 7. 1.

TABLE 7.1 Infusing UDL into Your CoP

CoP ACTIVITIES	ENGAGEMENT	REPRESENTATION	ACTION & EXPRESSION
Building relationships of mutual trust, reciprocity, and commitment	Employ approaches that minimize threats, facilitate coping skills, and heighten personal relevance.	Encourage mutual understanding by offering accessible, flexible choice in how information is shared.	Guide mutual goal-setting and foster shared progress monitoring strategies.
Learning and developing shared practice based on existing knowledge	Encourage use of mastery-oriented feedback, self-assessment, and self-reflection protocols.	Promote use of background knowledge and multiple options for representations, including visual, graphic, and digital.	Provide time and supportive tools for joint planning and strategy development.
Generating and discovering new knowledge	Promote high expectations for practitioners and learners.	Provide flexible options for transferring new knowledge to novel environments and contexts.	Offer graduated levels of scaffolds and support for changing instructional practice.
Taking purposeful action to produce shared resources	Match demands with supports, strategies, and resources.	Customize displays and offer flexible options for sharing resources.	Encourage choice and use accessible multimedia to share resources.

RECOGNITION Expand practices to create an integrated, system-wide approach to instruction and decision-making.

Scale 125

To scale your UDL initiative to a system-wide level, look for situations that will allow you to expand practices based on the UDL framework in both instructional and decision-making environments. You may be surprised by the options for creating system-wide participation that emerge as members of your UDL community (i.e., UDL-PLCs and UDL-CoPs) share their collaborative learning experiences with others.

Widen Your Sphere of Influence

During the Scale phase, you should explore ways to engage others who exist within your *sphere of influence.* Your sphere of influence consists of individuals and groups who may find the goals of your UDL action plan compelling or who have relationships with members of your UDL community. In a graphic display of your UDL community's sphere of influence, members of your UDL-CoP are located in the center of your sphere and non-participants are located in concentric circles that surround the center. Those located closest to center have stronger relationships or are closer in physical proximity. Those located in the outermost circles have weaker bonds or are physically farther away. Figure 7.1 illustrates how a UDL-CoP focused on UDL and high-school literacy might design key connections. In this example, members of the English, Media, Special Education, and English as a Second Language departments are represented in the center as the UDL-CoP. Because they also teach core academic subjects, members of the Science, Mathematics, and Social Studies departments are closely related to the UDL-CoP but not yet members. Other educators, such as teachers in the Physical Education, World Language, and Performing Arts departments, are in the next circle because weaker bonds exist between them and the members of the UDL-CoP. In the outermost circle are educators who have limited contact with the UDL-CoP members, such as those who teach in the elementary, middle, alternative, and charter schools.

If your initiative starts with one department, or a specific group within your school, you can expand by inviting in educators who occupy the next circle in your sphere. For instance, if your initial efforts have focused on improving literacy with the Language Arts and Special Education teachers, you can expand to include the science or STEM teachers. Or, if your project emphasizes building inclusive learning environments in early childhood classrooms, you can move on to multiple higher-grade levels. Or, if your UDL initiative addresses learner engagement at one school on your college campus, you can extend it to another school that's interested in aligning with your goals.

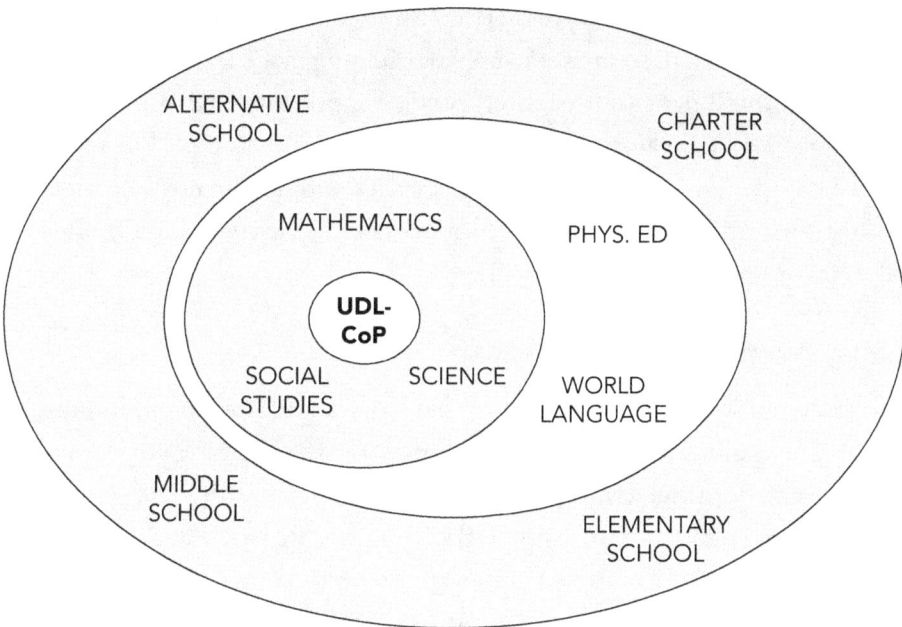

FIGURE 7.1: Sphere of Influence

It's Time to Recruit New Members

During the Scale phase, one key undertaking is recruiting new members for your UDL community. Review Chapter 6 for recruitment ideas. Search for new members who are open to reflecting on their beliefs, values, and practices and who are eager to make a change in their instruction. Investigate potential willingness and interest using the tools described in Chapter 4. Prepare all new members with learning sessions orienting them to your UDL community's shared vision and action plan and provide all new UDL-PLC members with the professional development needed to apply the UDL guidelines to their instruction.

Novice vs. Experienced

Some UDL projects have sought to engage educators who are new to the profession in their UDL implementation efforts only to find they become disengaged or frustrated a few months later. Novice educators typically need step-by-step rules or protocols, can be overly distracted by learner behaviors, and need more supervision than experienced or expert teachers (Dreyfus & Dreyfus, 1986). They certainly can benefit from learning about the UDL framework and participating in a UDL implementation initiative; however, you'll need to proactively provide supportive structures for them that more experienced educators may not need or want. This is a perfect example of learner variability, right? Two effective strategies for supporting novice educators are (1) pairing novices with experienced educators as PLC partners, and (2) offering additional time for one-on-one UDL coaching.

It's Time to Promote Your Work

During the Scale phase is a perfect time to learn more about how others are implementing UDL. In addition to observing classrooms or other learning environments within your system, consider visiting other systems—schools, districts, university campuses—that are engaged in infusing UDL into their instruction and decision-making processes. Also, make opportunities available to your current UDL community members to share their successes at local, state, regional, and national meetings. Increasingly, conference announcements are soliciting applications for presentations and seminars on successful change initiatives such as instructional transformation and UDL implementation. Of course, organizations that focus on UDL implementation, such as the UDL-IRN and CAST, host annual events specifically addressing UDL implementation. Your educators can expand their knowledge and improve their practice by becoming actively engaged in the international UDL community.

Encourage your UDL-PLC members to offer professional development and coaching for new departments or schools. Investigate ways to expand into other instructional domains. For example, several schools with UDL initiatives have included understanding of UDL in professional development sessions centered on positive behavior approaches and have successfully linked the UDL framework, especially the UDL principle of engagement, with their positive behavior programs.

Align with UDL, Not the Other Way Around

The experiences of the Bartholomew Consolidated School Corporation (BCSC) in Columbus, Indiana, provide an example of how to prioritize the UDL framework for system-wide decision-making. As knowledge of the UDL framework expanded throughout their system, BCSC did not want it to become just another project.

Instead, leadership advocated that UDL should be the overarching framework that informs all instructional decisions for the entire district. As they revised their district mission, their board of education adopted the UDL framework. One leader described their decision in this way: "UDL is no longer a district initiative, it is the framework through which all other initiatives, policies, and procedures are filtered, supported, and implemented" (Center on Technology and Disability, n.d., p. 3). Subsequently, if policies, processes, procedures, and structures didn't align with UDL, they were rejected because they were deemed as "not fitting" with their system's overarching framework.

MAKE IT ACTIONABLE Develop a graphic representation of your sphere of influence. Place your UDL community in the center and then draw several concentric circles around the center. Through collaborative discussions, determine which group(s) or learning environment(s) are adjacent to yours. Continue creating concentric circles until you have several circles in your sphere. Your sphere of influence will guide your decisions about how to move ahead during the Scale phase.

Beginning is easy; continuing, hard.

—JAPANESE PROVERB

ACTION AND EXPRESSION Infuse your policies, processes, procedures, and organizational structures with the UDL principles to make implementation more effective.

Seed Then Weed

As farmers know, plants will grow stronger and healthier if you broadly distribute seed and then gradually thin out weaker seedlings to allow the rest to have ample access to the sun and soil nutrients. In like manner, as you begin to "grow" and enhance your UDL initiative, look first for those organizational structures (i.e., The Four Ps: policies, processes, procedures, and practices) you believe to be strongly congruent with the shared vision articulated in your UDL action plan. (Revisit Chapter 6 if you need a refresher.) How can they be leveraged to support your efforts to scale your UDL initiative? Could projects or initiatives that serve only a few be reconstructed to benefit more learners? Could they be repurposed and infused with the UDL framework? How can you grow your UDL initiative by refocusing funding streams?

Weeding and thinning are also important as the enthusiastic UDL implementer in Figure 7.2 demonstrates. Reeves (2009) highlights the importance of "pulling the weeds" (i.e., unnecessary or ineffective programs and initiatives) to make time and energy available for what's worth doing.

FIGURE 7.2: Seed and weed   Illustration by Eli Brophy, Philadelphia, PA

During the Scale phase, you should identify which of the Four Ps in your system are failing to thrive or are impediments to change. Do they create hurdles or barriers? Do they prevent or limit your ability to grow your UDL initiative? For instance, are there unnecessary requirements about who can be included in certain learning environments or classrooms? Do programs, departments, or instructional practices restrict flexibility or choice in learner expression? Are there time-consuming procedures that can be completed more efficiently using technology?

Farmers understand how disruptive it can be to neighboring plants when you pull out established but unwanted weeds and how difficult it can be to shore up seedlings that are failing to thrive. Likewise, it's best to thwart unwanted or unsuccessful policies, processes, procedures, and practices before they become too entrenched. If they are linked to long-held beliefs about learners or are highly valued by even a few individuals, tread carefully. It may be difficult to cease or cut back tasks and other initiatives to make room for your UDL initiative's seedlings to grow. But it is necessary.

> *Educators are drowning under the weight of initiative fatigue—attempting to use the same amount of time, money, and emotional energy to accomplish more and more objectives.*
>
> —DOUGLAS B. REEVES, school leadership consultant

First Seed Inside Your UDL Circle

Principal Rene Sanchez of César Chávez High School in Houston, Texas, speaks about an epiphany that occurred toward the end of the first year of their UDL implementation initiative (Sanchez, Berquist, & Omelan, 2017). At that point, their team was contemplating next steps. Teachers and leaders were feeling more comfortable with the UDL framework but were having difficulty seeing connections between it and the myriad of other initiatives handed down from the district. After a scheduled set of UDL walkthroughs, the group's reflection was overshadowed by the recent unexpected death of a student. Sanchez realized that their mood illustrated the significance of engagement in the learning process. He also recognized that their future planning needed to use a new lens.

At the planning session, Sanchez drew an imaginary circle around the school explaining that "anything outside the circle that was not a component of teaching and learning should not be allowed to interfere with the process on the inside" (Sanchez et al., 2017, p. 108). Because UDL assigns importance to all three sets of learning networks (i.e., affective, recognition, and strategic networks) and offers significant support for developing affect as well as comprehension and expression skills, Sanchez viewed it differently than other district initiatives. At that moment, it was obvious that the other initiatives either needed to align with UDL or be diminished in priority.

Desirous of maintaining their focus inside the circle, the team's future planning targeted teaching and learning using the UDL framework. "UDL: Effective First Instruction" became the center of their circle. And, they also concluded that rather than waiting for someone outside their circle or school to align district expectations with their UDL initiative, the alignment between their school structures and UDL had to come from inside their circle—from the Chávez UDL implementation team.

Sanchez's epiphany is an exemplar for how a UDL lens can apply to your decision-making. All systems have a myriad of priorities that come from some other entity or groups that exist outside the circle. Using a laser focus on infusing UDL into your instruction will help your UDL community successfully wade through the clutter.

Let Evidence Lead the Way

Without evidence, decisions are based on guesswork. MacDonald (2013) urges teams to use data-driven dialogue to identify trends, patterns, and areas of need. She emphasizes: "Once a team begins to look at data together, priorities based on student needs and not teacher preferences emerge" (p. 95). When you developed your UDL action plan, you determined what evidence you would use to determine progress. (Refer to Chapter 5 for information on developing measurable outcomes for your UDL action plan.) You may have linked your measurable outcomes to survey results, learner outcome data, or information gleaned from observational rubrics. Make sure you consistently employ these tools and data for your decision-making throughout your implementation project.

As you scale your UDL initiative, it is critical that you use an evidentiary lens to make decisions about which policies, processes, procedures, and practices work and which don't. Patton and Patrizi (2010) suggest using cyclical data analysis that they refer to as "cycles of venturing, learning, and visioning" (p. 19). By utilizing dynamic data analysis, you may encounter some surprising insights along your UDL journey. However, there are also notable potholes to avoid. Be careful not to rely solely on aggregated data. Remember that the UDL framework is based on the premise that learners are variable. Because aggregates are averages, they do not evaluate growth at the individual learner's level. Disaggregating data into smaller groupings and evaluating personalized growth results over time will offer you the opportunity to dig deeper in determining the impact of your UDL initiative. In addition, taking a dynamic cyclical approach that examines data in smaller chunks will help you to resist the impulse to apply solutions with a broad brush to all learners.

> *I say, sir, that you can never make an intelligent judgment without evidence.*
>
> —MALCOLM X, Muslim minister and human rights activist

Inputs vs. Impact

To determine what to keep and what to thin, you need to measure policies, processes, procedures, and practices that result in long-term, direct, and indirect impact. Because systems change is complex and multilayered, direct cause and effect may not be apparent. In fact, outcomes of a transformative framework such as UDL can be unpredictable and progress may be nonlinear.

As mentioned in Chapter 5, don't get stuck in a factory mode of measurement that involves counting activities rather than evaluating learning. Latham (2014) recommends taking a hybrid developmental evaluation approach. Look for growth indicators in knowledge and skills and positive changes in beliefs, relationships, and mindsets. Instead of measuring what you do, assess what's been learned. Focus on finding patterns that can help you answer "how" and "why" questions. Collect ongoing evidence of changing attitudes and aspirations. Watch for leverage points that you can use to create shifts in your system. Evaluating authentic impact in this way will permit you to link what you learn about your UDL implementation to your future planning.

Develop and Utilize Formative Evaluation Protocols

Stiggins (2002) defines two types of learner assessments: (1) assessments *of* learning that are summative in nature, e.g., final exams and state standardized assessments, and (2) assessments *for* learning that are formative in nature because they are administered more than once and offer multiple opportunities to gauge growth over time, e.g., exit tickets and periodic surveys. Using this same paradigm for evaluating your implementation progress, you should incorporate formative types of measurements of your UDL action plan outcomes. By monitoring formative, ongoing measurements, your UDL community has the opportunity to make evidence-based decisions about how to enhance and scale UDL implementation. Examples of formative measurements of UDL implementation include learner and educator surveys, periodic interviews, learning walk observation tools based on rubrics, and self-reflection feedback.

Establishing formative evaluation protocols for your UDL implementation efforts is not only good practice, it also aligns with the UDL guidelines related to providing options for executive functions. To develop strategic, goal-directed learners, the UDL principle of action and expression recommends that we guide appropriate goal-setting, support planning, and strategy development, and that we enhance capacity for monitoring progress.

WATCH FOR UDL

Selected Action and Expression Engagement Guidelines

- Provide options for executive functions.
    - ▶ Guide appropriate goal-setting.
    - ▶ Support planning and strategy development.
    - ▶ Enhance capacity for monitoring progress.

© CAST, 2014. Used with permission.

MAKE IT ACTIONABLE During the Scale phase, you should carefully assess what's working and what isn't. Revisit "Spotlight 6.3: Evaluating the Four Ps" in Chapter 6 with an eye toward "thinning" or eliminating ineffective, inefficient structures and those determined to be barriers.

WHAT DO WE DO NOW?

During the Scale phase, your UDL-CoP should reexamine the Who, What, and How of your UDL implementation action plan:

Who: To uncover new opportunities to grow your UDL initiative, extend your UDL initiative to other parts of your sphere of influence by inviting new participants into your UDL collaborative community. Be sure they are oriented to your UDL shared vision and action plan.

What: To increase your impact, assess the array of UDL instructional practices your UDL-PLC members are currently using with an eye toward adding new strategies (i.e., what). Ask your UDL-PLC members to assess their application of the UDL framework and select at least one untried guideline to explore. Continue to add UDL practices to their repertoire as your UDL-PLC members demonstrate readiness. Provide the professional development and UDL coaching they need to expand their UDL practices.

How: Augment and intensify your outcomes, enhance resources and supports, and eliminate those structures (i.e., The Four Ps) that are barriers to success. Gather ongoing evidence and look for patterns to show how instruction infused with UDL is transforming your system.

ESSENTIAL QUESTIONS

1. Who else might be interested in implementing UDL?
2. To what extent can others help us achieve the goals of our UDL action plan?
3. What emerging roles are available for UDL-CoP members?
4. To what extent can our UDL initiative benefit other learners, educators, stakeholders, or the community as a whole?
5. What are the most important elements of our collaborative community to recognize and expand to other environments?
6. In what ways can we support technical aspects of the evolving policies, processes, procedures, and practices of our UDL-CoP?
7. What are the key policies, processes, procedures, and practices that need to be shared with newly established implementation environments or sites?
8. How can we grow our UDL implementation practices into other learning environments?

WHAT'S NEXT? Chapter 8 discusses how to optimize your UDL implementation efforts.

8

Optimize

GUIDING QUESTIONS

- To what extent are UDL characteristics inherent in your learning culture?
- How can iterative data analysis help you optimize UDL implementation?
- What does the future hold for your UDL implementation?

LET'S HEAR FROM BARTHOLOMEW CONSOLIDATED SCHOOL CORPORATION (BCSC) IN INDIANA AND MONTGOMERY COUNTY PUBLIC SCHOOLS (MCPS) IN MARYLAND.

After more than a decade of UDL implementation, the Bartholomew Consolidated School Corporation (BCSC) is concentrating on optimizing UDL by focusing on continuous refinement and improvement. UDL in BCSC is not just a tool for designing learning environments, unit plans, or lessons; it is a framework that enhances an existing culture that values inclusion and celebrates variability. In BCSC, the UDL framework is *the foundation* for all decision-making. Throughout this chapter, you will hear from Director of Special Education George van Horn from BCSC about how the district has optimized UDL, including cultivating a learning organization committed to enhancing UDL practice and using UDL as a basis for their teacher evaluation process, ensuring that UDL is part of their hiring practices. You'll also hear from High Incidence Accessible Technology (HIAT) Specialist Bill McGrath from Montgomery County Public Schools (MCPS) in Maryland, about how a district of over 200 schools is working to optimize UDL implementation from the bottom up.

OPTIMIZE

The Optimize phase is aptly titled because it is all about enhancing and optimizing your UDL implementation. During this phase, UDL implementation is not viewed as a project or initiative within your system; it is routine—the modus operandi for how your system works. As HIAT Specialist Bill McGrath describes UDL after a decade of implementation work: "Now, UDL is just part of how we do business."

The Optimize phase is characterized by *continuous improvement*, innovation, and refinement, and its purpose is maximizing the sustainability of UDL as a system-wide decision-making and instructional framework. Pathways during the Optimize phase include

- *nurturing a UDL culture* throughout your system,

- *maximizing improvement* by embedding practices and iterative processes that balance stability with innovation, and

- strategically *predicting, responding, and planning* for internal and external changes that could impact UDL implementation.

OPTIMIZE
- Nurture UDL Culture
- Maximize Improvement
- Predict and Respond

ENGAGEMENT Nurture a UDL culture throughout your system.

Nurture a UDL Culture

Culture is a complex construct. When humans gather, it is always present. It permeates through every group. Even when we are not attending to it, we *feel* it. Culture is often associated with specific group identities, such as ethnic, social, or socioeconomic, but it also exists in organizations, work situations, and learning environments.

In 2001, Hall and Hord defined an organization's culture as the "individually and socially constructed values, norms, and beliefs about an organization and how it should behave . . ." (p. 194). A definition of culture that aligns well with the three UDL principles is ". . . shared patterns of behaviors and interactions, cognitive constructs, and affective understandings" (Center for Advanced Research on Language Acquisition, 2009, p. 1). Reeves (2009) defines culture as simply "the way we do things around here" (p.37), and Aguilar (2016) says that culture is really about "people" (p. 264). For our purposes, we view *culture* as the shared assumptions, attitudes, and learned behavior that determine what happens within a learning environment.

Dimensions of Culture

It's easy to portray a specific culture by identifying obvious attributes, such as clothing, food, and music. However, this superficial characterization doesn't really help address when you are talking about the culture that exists in a classroom, school, university, organization, or other system. In reality, culture is multilayered. Hildalgo (1993) describes three elements—concrete, behavioral, and symbolic—that are helpful in explaining the multidimensional aspects of the culture within a typical learning environment or system:

> **Concrete.** This is the most visible and tangible characteristic of culture. Composed of mostly surface-level features, it is evident in *what* you can see or hear in your learning environment. As you look around the walls or structures, you'll see representations of academic content and items that learners use to express themselves. Concrete elements are most often illustrated in how you celebrate or recognize your achievements.

Behavioral. Steeped in what you value, this component of culture clarifies how you define your interactions and social roles, including how you communicate and engage with learners and educators, both verbally and nonverbally. Behavioral aspects reflect the policies, practices, and structures that dictate *how* you do what you do in your learning environment.

Symbolic. This dimension of culture can be abstract, but it is probably the most important level because it clarifies how individuals within the learning environment define themselves. Symbolic attributes are often transmitted through the stories we tell. Emanating from your expectations, beliefs, mindset, rituals, and customs, symbolic elements are the basis for *why* you do what you do.

Moving Toward a UDL Culture

Like any other culture, a UDL culture is built over time. If you have been moving through the UDL phases, you should be well on your way to creating your UDL culture. As discussed in previous chapters, educators and learners in a *UDL climate* hold high expectations, respect variability, promote accessibility and flexibility, and value the contributions of all learners (see Chapter 5). These aspirations create the foundation for the symbolic dimensions of your UDL culture. In a *UDL community*, members have joint authentic experiences, build collaborative structures, and value shared learning (see Chapter 7). These interactions form the behavioral aspects of your UDL culture.

All of Hidalgo's three dimensions of culture (i.e., concrete, behavioral, and symbolic) are evident in a UDL culture. Educators and learners in a *UDL culture* routinely celebrate variability and collective learning, display their commitment to continuous improvement, and nurture a growth mindset.

> **REFLECTION** As humans, we tell stories about what's important to us. Your UDL culture will have its own story. What is it? Capture your journey. Share it.

Learning Is at the Core

A learning organization is at the core of a UDL culture. What do we mean by a *learning organization?* Senge (1990) first popularized the term to describe a business that facilitated the learning of all its workers and continually transformed itself. Aguilar (2016) recently defined a learning organization as "an organization in which everyone is learning" (p.185). This description aligns well with a learning environment that has adopted UDL as its guiding framework. Everyone—students, educators, administrators, community members—is viewed as a learner within a UDL culture. Since all learning is the result of our interaction with context (Rose, Rouhani, & Fischer, 2013), your UDL culture creates the context for learning for both educators and learners.

Example from the Field

Van Horn offers an example from BCSC: "To cultivate and enhance a UDL culture, BCSC staff is committed to becoming a learning organization. District leaders design and deliver professional learning that moves beyond application of UDL in classrooms and applies the framework to educator experiences as learners themselves" (G. van Horn, personal interview, July 2018). In modeling UDL in adult learning experiences, BCSC further demonstrates its commitment to application of the UDL framework in all learning environments—those designed for adults and those designed for children.

Address Deeper Negative Issues

Keep in mind that the culture of any environment is reflected in how people behave. In truth, the culture in some systems is hostile, unhealthy, dysfunctional, or even toxic. It could take a very long time to transform a culture that is this negative into a UDL culture that celebrates variability, flexibility, and shared learning. Without significant changes in the community's underlying beliefs and values, successful UDL implementation is unlikely. In fact, if you don't address these deeper cultural issues first, you may go through the motions of implementation, maybe see some superficial changes, but you will not be able to reach sustainable transformation (MacDonald, 2013).

> **MAKE IT ACTIONABLE** How will you know if you've established a UDL culture? Although you may begin to *feel* it, you can also specifically look for multidimensional aspects of a UDL culture within your system. Review Table 8.1, which illustrates examples of how concrete, behavioral, and symbolic aspects of culture intersect with the UDL guidelines.

TABLE 8.1: Crosswalk of the UDL Framework with Aspects of Culture

ENGAGEMENT	RECOGNITION	ACTION AND EXPRESSION
CONCRETE		
Demands are balanced by resources.	Learners and educators employ strategies for information processing (e.g., visual charts, calendars, photo schedules, routines).	Learners and educators employ effective strategies for recalling, analyzing, and synthesizing information.
Learners and educators exercise choice over salient aspects of teaching and learning.	Content is displayed using accessible options for auditory and visual information.	All learners and educators can navigate comfortably through the physical space of the learning environment.
BEHAVIORAL		
Learners and educators feel safe and can focus on learning.	Instruction emphasizes interdisciplinary relationships and critical thinking strategies (e.g., comparing, contrasting).	Learners and educators exhibit problem-solving and strategic planning skills (e.g., hypothesizing, predicting, prioritizing).
Learners and educators contribute to effective, shared collaborative learning.	All educators teach content-related vocabulary and language structures across learning environments.	Instruction engages learners in various types of authentic discussions and debates.
Learners and educators employ effective strategies for increasing emotional intelligence.	Text, mathematical notation, and symbols are displayed using accessible, culturally responsive multimedia.	Learners and educators express knowledge using accessible, flexible multimedia tools.
SYMBOLIC		
Learners and educators set high expectations and express the belief that everyone can learn.	Learners and educators leverage cultural backgrounds and experiences for learning.	Learners and educators employ effective strategies for authentic goal-setting and personalized planning.
Decisions are based on collaborative community self-reflection.	Interdisciplinary, integrated instruction promotes knowledge transfer and generalization.	Ongoing assessments of progress illustrate a growth mindset among learners and educators.

ENGAGEMENT	RECOGNITION	ACTION AND EXPRESSION
Learners and educators express pride in their learning achievements and identify as expert learners.	Common scaffolds and flexible instructional techniques exist across learning environments.	Decisions allow for practice and gradual demonstration of proficiency among learners and educators.
Feedback to learners and educators is mastery-oriented based on a growth mindset.	Multilingual, culturally responsive techniques are valued and embedded in instruction.	Inclusive learning environments are enhanced by the use of accessible tools and assistive technologies.

RECOGNITION Embed processes and structures that allow for innovation while maximizing continuous improvement.

Maximize Continuous Improvement

Sustaining and optimizing meaningful transformation is a long-term process. What do we mean by *optimizing*? You'll need to purposefully apply the innovative aspects of your UDL initiative system-wide to maximize its positive impact. However, new processes and structures cannot be just grafted on the old system. In fact, systems-change expert Kim (2001) cautions against assuming that what worked before will continue to work. He adds that simply extrapolating to a larger scale is a perilous approach to sustainability. Instead, a critical step during the Optimize phase is adopting a continuous improvement mindset that involves careful, growth-oriented reflection.

Example from the Field

In a UDL culture, people see themselves affected by and mirrored in the ongoing change within their environment and they make building positive relationships and transforming learning a daily endeavor. For instance, BCSC viewed maximizing improvement as dependent on growing UDL practices among educators system-wide. Using a growth mindset, they actively looked for ways to shape and improve practices. They realized that effective UDL practices had to be embedded in the daily instruction of every classroom. Consequently, the district developed a number of processes that *maximize continuous improvement*, including adopting a revised teacher evaluation tool and creating supports for optimizing teacher impact. Fifty percent of their revised teacher evaluation is based on implementation of UDL in the learning environment. In addition, to support teacher growth, not only in core content but also in how to best refine their practice and design flexible learning environments, each school is assigned a UDL facilitator. Facilitators meet regularly with teachers utilizing an instructional coaching cycle to encourage continual reflection of teaching practices aligned with the UDL guidelines.

> *Sustainability is more than a victory in an endurance contest. . . . True sustainability requires a double-edged focus on people and practices*
>
> —DOUGLAS B. REEVES, education leadership consultant

Iterative Benefit Analysis

What does continuous improvement look like in a growth-oriented learning environment? According to Fullan (2001), embedding continuous improvement starts with reexamining your "moral purpose" and then consistently evaluating and reevaluating meaningful results. In an iterative way, you use the data from your review to refine your planned outcomes, identify potential barriers, and enhance your professional learning strategies. Repeated examination of your UDL implementation plan should track the benefits of your project, including whether

- you are being effective.
- your outcomes are authentic.
- your actions are in sync with accomplishing your shared vision.

A note of caution: Your UDL implementation journey reflection should not be based on a dogmatic sorting mindset because a rigid yes-no review can cause you to inadvertently throw away policies, processes, procedures, or practices that are *not yet* showing significant impact but are still indicators of progress. Instead, look for trends or patterns that are moving in the right direction.

To be effective, your cycle of continuous improvement should include the following seven steps repeated in a purposefully iterative manner (see Figure 8.1):

1. Review your implementation plan goals.
2. Identify indicators of progress.
3. Analyze both educator and learner data looking for trends and patterns.
4. Uncover gaps and potential hurdles.
5. Refine your goals, policies, processes, procedures, and practices as needed.
6. Enhance practices by providing professional learning and coaching.
7. Return to reviewing your implementation plan goals.

Like BCSC, if you use a growth mindset to add supports to structures and strategies that are not quite there yet, you can reasonably expect sustained success.

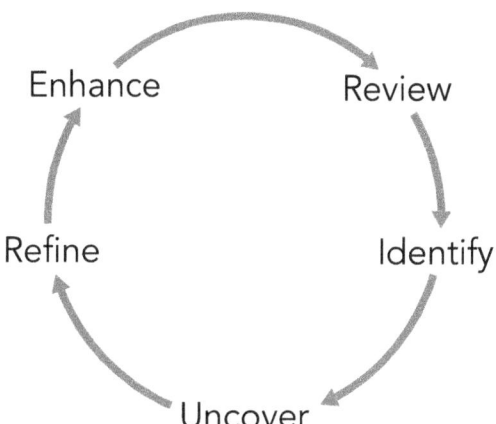

FIGURE 8.1: Optimizing through a cycle of continuous improvement

Measure Growth and Progress

Conducting regular evaluations during the Optimize phase can help identify facilitators of success and potential barriers to progress and can allow you to make iterative strategy adjustments. Your progress assessment should be based on authentic data and suit your system and culture. Nonetheless, avoiding rigid assessments that do not allow you to infuse flexibility and choice into your iterative review can be a formidable challenge. Many evaluation processes are too rigid to measure progress or detect subtle changes in beliefs, values, or instructional practices. For instance, most summative evaluations are designed to judge the final effectiveness or benefits of a project, and they are typically conducted after the project is in full operation by external evaluators who may not have a deep understanding of UDL. Such evaluations do not offer the opportunity for continual adjustments and are not flexible enough to permit review of the key factors or impact of your UDL implementation initiative. Instead, choose flexible assessments that will provide you with ongoing measures of learner and educator experiences.

Example from the Field

The school improvement process utilized by the Montgomery County Public Schools (MCPS) aligns well with UDL implementation because it encourages multiple measurements of student growth. According to HIAT Specialist Bill McGrath, this process creates varied measures of student performance and more ways of monitoring the effects of UDL implementation in the classroom, school, and district. McGrath explains:

> *It is not just state testing data. We use curriculum-based measures on a week-to-week and month-to-month basis which gives validation to student engagement and what students and parents are saying. So, when I think of how we measure UDL I think that it is the same as how we measure school improvement—it's the same as how we measure any change. We use "varied measures" (B. McGrath, personal interview, September 2018).*

MAKE IT ACTIONABLE Assessments of continuous improvement can guide a thorough examination of your progress. Like MCPS, your system may already be using an adaptable evaluation process that can be applied to your UDL implementation efforts. In addition to employing available learner performance data, your UDL-CoP may want to use systems change measurement strategies (M. Hargreaves, 2010). The most suitable processes for UDL implementation projects are these:

Developmental evaluations provide rapid feedback on activities that can be observed by an evaluator (or a set of evaluators) who has a collaborative relationship with your UDL community of practice (CoP) and functions as a member of your team. Using a rubric or set of expectations, the evaluator shares observations of the CoP in action. The rubric should be generated by your UDL-CoP, be aligned with your UDL implementation plan, and authentically measure your expected outcomes.

Formative evaluations are often conducted periodically by individuals who are not members of your UDL-CoP but who have a deep understanding of UDL. Formative evaluations identify strengths and weaknesses, detect unexpected gaps and glitches in the system, and look at the progress your UDL-CoP is making over time toward accomplishing your plan's goals.

Program monitoring and accountability evaluations are designed specifically to monitor projects; they track process and outcome measures through management information systems. Monitoring focuses on identified indicators that are reviewed and updated periodically as your implementation plan evolves.

These three evaluation processes are sensitive to the multifaceted aspects of your UDL implementation plan and can be adapted to meet your needs.

ACTION AND EXPRESSION Strategically predict and plan for internal and external changes that could impact UDL implementation.

Predict and Plan

As you develop structures for continuous improvement during the Optimize phase, it's important to build in opportunities to predict potential as-yet-unrealized barriers and turns in the road that can slow or halt your UDL journey. Certain gaps or miscalculations in your UDL implementation plan and unforeseen changes can create unanticipated hurdles to your optimizing efforts.

> *The best way to predict the future is to create it.*
>
> —PETER DRUCKER, American management consultant

Predict What Could Be

Educational institutions are both stable and chaotic at the same time. Long-term planning can be turned on its head quickly by changes in personnel, budget, or mission-focus. During the Optimize phase, you should take time to predict what could happen to derail your UDL implementation plan over time. This is similar to knowing about learner variability: if you can reasonably anticipate that something might occur, you can plan for it. It doesn't have to be an event that will result in complete abandonment of your goals, but any impasse that could have a significant negative or positive impact should be considered as you review and revise your implementation plan.

Scenario Planning

Originally used for health-reform implementation, scenario planning offers a way for your UDL-CoP to break away from traditional problem-solving approaches to investigate potential changes and challenges. Snow, Lynn, and Beer (2015) define scenario planning as "a process for building flexibility into strategy by surfacing several possible futures and then exploring how strategic decisions might play out under different conditions" (p. 13). By prospectively investigating potential blind spots and unplanned deviations, you claim collective responsibility for possible futures and purposefully prepare for them.

Scenario planning can also help you to discover the *drivers* within your system—those levers within your system that encourage or impede change (Snow, et al., 2015). Some drivers can contribute to improvements and positive growth. Examples include job-embedded, quality professional learning, mentoring, and coaching. Other drivers, such as a need to maintain the status quo, can be obstructions. Being mindful of your system's drivers will enable your UDL-CoP to prepare for potential futures more effectively.

What barriers could have a significant effect on your UDL implementation plan? Consider the potential impacts of the following:

- Unreasonable expectations or timeline

- No clearly identified need to change

- Unaddressed fear underlying a pervasive system-wide reluctance to change

- Unrealized positive outcomes that lead to disappointment

- Incomplete or mismatched assessments that lead to initiative fatigue

- Significant changes in leadership or support

- Major new initiatives that impede or interfere with your plan

- Loss or addition of personnel critical to your success

- Loss or increase in funding or resources

WATCH FOR UDL

Selected Action and Expression Engagement Guidelines

- Provide options for executive functions.
  - ▶ Guide appropriate goal-setting.
  - ▶ Support planning and strategy development.
  - ▶ Enhance capacity for monitoring progress.

© CAST, 2014. Used with permission.

Example from the Field

The leadership team in BCSC strategically *predicts and plans* for internal and external changes that could impact UDL implementation. When the long-time superintendent retired, district leaders ensured that all prospective candidates understood UDL and its relationship to district expectations. By reinforcing this emphasis in the application process, district leaders made it clear that regardless of who holds the highest office in the district, that person must espouse the core beliefs of the UDL framework in their work.

Leadership as a Driver

Drivers within any system are those components that can and do impact change (Fixsen, et al., 2005). The leadership structures of your system and your UDL implementation team are critical implementation drivers. In actuality, the rate and steadiness of optimizing your implementation can depend on how the leadership of your system is structured and managed.

Burnes (2004) points out that education institutions are complex systems that typically have *top-down leadership*, meaning that authorized decision-making, control, and communication come from an individual or set of individuals, such as a superintendent, other administrators, or board at the top of the management pyramid. In contrast, decision-making and control in a *bottom-up leadership* organization tends to be diffused, coming from individuals or self-organizing teams at the bottom of the management pyramid. Independent charter schools, small nonprofit colleges, and community early childhood programs are often self-organizing organizations with a bottom-up leadership structure.

Both top-down and bottom-up leadership structures can bring about instructional transformation. Without paying significant attention to building a collaborative community, implementation projects with a top-down leadership structure may encounter limitations, such as educator resistance and "contrived collegiality" as described by A. Hargreaves (1994; see Chapter 6). Likewise, because they may lack the empowerment to make timely decisions, implementation projects with a bottom-up leadership structure may face crucial structural hurdles and their rate of change may be slower.

Systems-change guru Andy Hargreaves suggests that a *horizontal* leadership structure—which includes elements from both top-down and bottom-up structures—offers sustainable leadership for continuous improvement (Datnow, 2011; A. Hargreaves, 1994; Hargreaves & Fink, 2009). A horizontal leadership structure brings together UDL-CoP members from different positions within the organization to efficiently and effectively optimize success. Those UDL-CoP members who are administrators and decision makers can remove outside barriers and offer financial support, and members who are empowered practitioners and classroom educators can directly impact learners. If your team experiences recurring impediments to implementation progress, you may want to rethink the leadership structure of your UDL-CoP. Adding leaders who can leverage change or empowered practitioners with decision-making authority may be solutions worth exploring.

Example from the Field

For MCPS, UDL implementation is not a top-down initiative. Instead, it began when the HIAT team took it upon themselves to help educators across the district learn about UDL after the state of Maryland established state regulations requiring that districts ensure that all teachers understand the UDL framework and that curricula align with it. McGrath observes

> *We are not an implementation team that has a mandate. We are a consolidation team that has adopted the responsibility of helping teachers to learn about UDL and connect with UDL implementation efforts within the district (B. McGrath, personal interview, September 2018).*

After a decade of concerted efforts, McGrath and his team are empowered and able to leverage system-wide changes that impact UDL implementation at what McGrath calls "deeper" levels. For example, as the school library media staff looked into ordering new resources, the HIAT team helped them match their purchases with the UDL framework and identified curriculum and instruction needs related to UDL and accessibility. McGrath adds: "We are the connectors. We make connections to help them do their jobs better" (B. McGrath personal interview, September 2018).

MAKE IT ACTIONABLE To optimize your implementation efforts, begin by nurturing your UDL culture. Create and share stories of individual and community successes that capture the enthusiasm and triumphs of your UDL team members, including your UDL-PLC members' use of best practices. Consider using digital means to share your UDL journey. Telling the story of your UDL journey will add to your momentum. Be sure to honor accomplishments by designing activities that award recognition and praise. Such events encourage engagement, sustain effort, and recruit interest among those who may be curious but reluctant.

In addition to formal regular evaluations of your UDL implementation plan, conduct focus groups, interviews, surveys, and other data collection activities to assess and measure the ongoing success of your project. Engage UDL community members in your progress monitoring so that they can assess their individual progress as well. Use authentic data for your iterative analysis and optimization of your UDL implementation plan.

Scenarios are not predictions. However, scenario planning can help your UDL-CoP build bridges between your current implementation strategies and the future of your implementation plan. Strategically prepare for future impediments and achievements.

WHAT DO WE DO NOW?

Scenario planning is actually storytelling based on potential future events. To complete your scenarios, refer to Spotlight 8.1.

SPOTLIGHT 8.1:
Scenario Planning

Convene your UDL-CoP to collectively contemplate the following steps:

1. **Map what is.** Initially, your UDL-CoP maps your current plans over an extended timeline, perhaps several years. While you do this, identify those factors that serve as facilitators of success undergirding your plan. What are the implementation drivers in your system? What can you reasonably expect to happen in the next year? In the year after that? And so on.

2. **Ask what if.** Through collective consensus your team builds an understanding of potential futures by responding to *"What if?"* questions. For instance:
   ▸ What if we continue as is without any changes?
   ▸ What if funding changes?
   ▸ What if leadership changes?
   ▸ What if there are competing mandates?
   ▸ What if the system reorganizes?

3. **Identify what could be.** Examine and uncover internal and external risks to successful implementation and optimizing your impact over time. Ask *"What could be?"* As you review the potential risks, divide them into three categories: (1) those that are outside your control or sphere of influence, (2) those that are relatively well understood so their effects can be anticipated, and (3) those that are not familiar and therefore loaded with uncertainties.

4. **Determine if - then.** Develop potential scenarios that account for the adjustments you'll need to make to address the risks you've uncovered. Your team should respond to *"If this happens, we can . . . ."* Even those risks that are outside your control may have a potential response.

5. **Embed predictions.** As much as feasible, compare your current plan and strategies (i.e., *What is*) with your predictions (i.e., *If - then*). Redefine as needed to embed flexibility and options that will address impediments you might encounter as you move forward on your UDL journey.

ESSENTIAL QUESTIONS

1. To what extent are your system's values and beliefs nurtured and demonstrated in your culture?

2. How are learners and educators recognized and rewarded for their contributions?

3. To what extent do individual work products contribute to achieving your UDL community goals?

4. What would your system be like if continuous improvement was expected?

5. How can you prepare for internal or external factors that can affect future implementation efforts?

WHAT'S NEXT? Chapter 9 offers a call to action for the UDL field.

9

Beyond Implementation

GUIDING QUESTIONS

- How fast can we move?
- What funding sources are available?
- How can we add to what others are doing?
- To what extent can we impact the growing UDL field?

LEARNING THAT'S NEVER-ENDING

The most amazing aspect of UDL implementation is that you are always learning. Even those individuals who have been dubbed UDL Rockstars and UDL Experts readily admit they are constantly learning about new ways to address implementation and novel aspects of the UDL framework that they hadn't considered before. In many ways the UDL journey is a never-ending journey. You may find this frightening. It is also exhilarating!

Where Are They Now?

How fast you move on your UDL journey will depend on your ability to anticipate or avoid major disruptive influences and the constancy of your leadership. One key way to drive your momentum in the beginning is to find those early adopters to help you build a cadre of UDL enthusiasts. They can bolster your progress, particularly at the Integrate and Scale phases. In addition, consistent, authentic professional learning can be the difference between your UDL journey oozing along as a slow-moving trickle of change or spreading like a transformational river.

It's helpful to consider how others have progressed. In 2012, the UDL implementation project funded by the Bill and Melinda Gates Foundation highlighted the work of several school districts that were at different points with UDL implementation (Ganley & Ralabate, 2013). Each district approached their journey differently. Cecil County public schools in Maryland were just beginning to explore UDL as a framework that might intersect with their literacy program. Following the UDL implementation project, the district participated in a multiyear federally funded project that included professional development on the application of UDL. Their change efforts moved steadily through initial exploration to integration and scaling.

Chapter 6 highlighted the UDL journey for the Baltimore County Public Schools (BCPS), a large public school district in Maryland. Although BCPS had provided professional development sessions focused on UDL for many years prior to their involvement in the UDL project, large-scale change in practice was not evident (Ganley & Ralabate, 2013). At the beginning of the UDL project, they were moving from the Prepare phase to the Integrate phase. Their work with this project caused BCPS leadership to conclude that creating and supporting professional learning communities (PLCs) focused on UDL (UDL-PLCs) was a more effective route for them (Burke, 2017). The collaborative nature of their UDL-PLCs significantly hastened their UDL implementation across content areas, grade levels, and schools. Today, they continue to scale and optimize UDL implementation throughout their district emphasizing instructional transformation and responsive instruction. Their end goal is equitable access for all learners.

WHISTLE-STOP To learn more about Baltimore County Public School's instructional transformation, visit *http://www.bcps.org/academics/HowWeTeach/what_learning_looks_like.html*.

Bartholomew Consolidated School Corporation (BCSC) is recognized as a pioneer in systemic UDL implementation. Their UDL journey was reviewed in Chapters 1 and 8. When they joined the UDL implementation project in 2012, they were already providing professional learning focused on UDL to all educators in their district using professional learning workshops and instructional coaching. At that time, they were interested in enhancing their efforts to scale and optimize UDL implementation (Ganley & Ralabate, 2013). BCSC continues its optimizing efforts today. The UDL framework is foundational for decision-making and integral to their school culture. They not only provide professional learning for their own staff, but they host a UDL conference every summer that is attended by UDL enthusiasts from throughout the country. In addition, scores of educators from across the globe visit their classrooms every year to observe UDL in action.

Some systems try to model their UDL implementation project after what others have done. This may work and it may not. Your system is unique; so, your UDL journey will be unique. Learn from what others have done and apply what fits. The communities of each of the districts discussed in this book exemplified various values, needs, and resources. Each was at a different point along the implementation continuum and each took a distinct path toward systemic transformation. So will you.

FLEXIBLE SOLUTIONS TO FUNDING BARRIERS

Limited funding is probably the most common barrier experienced by systems as they chart their UDL journey. Even finding monies for professional development, teacher planning, or attendance at conferences can be challenging.

Braid UDL with Other Funding Initiatives

At this time, no national funding sources in the US offer financial resources specifically for UDL implementation initiatives. Instead, look for state and local opportunities that align with your UDL implementation goals. Consider the following ideas:

- State or local funding sources are often targeted toward priorities associated with curriculum redesign or expanded access to technology. Look for ways you can authentically integrate these priorities with your UDL project goals.

- Special education funds have been a reliable source for funding UDL initiatives at state and local levels. Whenever Congress reauthorizes the Individuals with Disabilities Education Act (IDEA), it highlights funding priorities. For example, in 2004, the IDEA funding priorities included "Results-Driven Accountability," which was aimed at improving results for students with disabilities. Instructional changes based on UDL can and do expand access to inclusive learning environments, and drive improved outcomes for all learners, including students with disabilities. As a matter of fact, UDL professional learning has been identified by local and state school leaders as a high-impact strategy, frequently linked with other educational initiatives and often supported by special education program funds (Ralabate et al., 2012).

- Title I funds under the Elementary and Secondary Education Act (ESEA, now the ESSA) are typically targeted for specific schools in low-income areas or for groups of students who are impacted by poverty. Key changes made in 2015 when Congress reauthorized ESEA as the Every Student Succeeds Act (ESSA) may offer your system funding opportunities. ESSA encouraged states and districts to adhere to the principles of UDL as they develop assessment and accountability plans, implement technology projects, and create programs for comprehensive literacy instruction. Associating your UDL implementation plan with initiatives that address student assessment, technology, or literacy can offer your UDL project an important source of funding (CAST, 2016).

- Title III of the ESEA addresses programs for English learners (ELs) and funding for professional learning about effective English language instruction. Providing all educators with professional learning opportunities focused on UDL will not only boost the progress of ELs, but it will also build collaborative, academically challenging, and inclusive learning environments for all learners.

WHISTLE-STOP For more information on the intersection of culturally responsive teaching and UDL, see Ralabate & Nelson's book *Culturally Responsive Design for English Learners: The UDL Approach* (2017).

- Many states have forged ahead with state-level UDL implementation and some have established financial incentives for local or regional UDL projects. For instance, the Wisconsin Department of Public Instruction partnered with CAST and provided funding for UDL Startup Grants, and regional centers in Texas are supporting schools and districts that are offering professional learning focused on UDL and inclusive practices.

- Raise awareness and foster a sense of commitment within your system. Local businesses are often interested in ways to invest in changes in their schools that can be transformative. Look for influential parents or school board members who will see the potential that UDL offers and can be champions for your UDL initiative. Meet with them and share your goals and ideas. Share the successful UDL journeys of others. Directly ask local community leaders to help you to raise the funding you need to successfully accomplish your UDL implementation plan.

- Internationally, UDL implementation is funded in a variety of ways. Often associated with inclusive education practices, UDL initiatives are endorsed and financially supported by professional associations, universities, and governments across the globe, including Australia, Canada, England, Finland, Italy, New Zealand, Norway, Singapore, South Africa, Sweden, and the United Arab Emirates. Just one example is the recently announced initiative of the Association of Higher Education Access and Disability (AHEAD) in Dublin, Ireland, aimed at promoting inclusive learning environments through the implementation of UDL.

These are just a few examples of potential funding opportunities. To find funding for your UDL project, you'll need to be responsive to what already exists and be flexible in your thinking.

BUILD UDL EXPERTISE

To build a deep understanding of UDL implementation among your team members, look for ways to learn from others who have embarked upon their own UDL journeys. Action steps to consider include connecting with recognized UDL experts and pursuing research opportunities.

Join the UDL Experts

You'll recall that the ultimate goal of UDL implementation is to create expert learners. *Expert learners* are knowledgeable, understand how they learn, and are motivated to learn more (see Chapter 1). Both students and educators develop into expert learners as the result of effective UDL implementation. In fact, if you aren't already, you and your team are well on your way to becoming UDL experts. *UDL experts* augment the description of *expert learner* by adding the desire to teach others about the UDL framework and UDL implementation. *Your UDL team's deepening expertise can inspire others.* As successful UDL implementation spreads across the US and around the globe, the list of UDL enthusiasts continues to expand. These are some ways you can connect with others who are passionate about UDL implementation:

- Attend the annual symposium and conferences hosted by CAST and the UDL-IRN (see *http://castprofessionallearning.org/project/casts-annual-udl-symposium/* and *https://summit.udl-irn.org/*)

- Participate in free webinars on UDL implementation (see *http://castprofessional learning.org/free-udl-webinars/* and *https://www.ocali.org/project/udl-webinars*)

- Engage in online UDL chats, such as *http://twubs.com/udlchat* and #UDLHE

Discover UDL Research Opportunities

Rigorous research that can help guide UDL implementation is surfacing, but it is slow-going. Because the framework emphasizes flexibility and learner choice, UDL does not fit easily into a typical research standard that requires rigid fidelity while applying specified protocols to experimental and control groups. Some UDL researchers are successfully publishing studies that use qualitative and mixed measures. In addition, iteratively evaluating progress and growth over time offers promising research opportunities. The measures you are using to assess your UDL implementation initiative could hold a treasure trove of raw data for UDL researchers. As a matter of fact, research organizations and higher education institutions are always on the look-out for partners who can help them frame research questions and lead them to UDL-related data. *Your UDL team's discoveries can help design the future of UDL implementation.*

To add to the field of UDL implementation research, consider offering researchers the opportunity to study your system. Here are a few sites to get you started:

- CAST Research: *http://www.cast.org/work-with-us/research.html#.W8ttAfZFwmI*
- UDL-IRN Research: *https://udl-irn.org/research/*

Share Your UDL Journey

Whether you realize it or not, you've got something worth sharing! Your UDL journey can be an inspiration to someone else who is trying to figure out how to get started, how to keep their momentum going, or how to get past a recent hurdle. You may have the answer. You and your team have learned a lot about what works and what doesn't. Since the UDL framework is based on what research tells us about how humans learn, it is systematic and predictable. Likewise, you can reasonably expect your experiences to intersect with what other UDL implementers are learning. And, because UDL implementation encourages flexibility and unique choices, you may have selected an unconventional approach or implementation strategy that is the perfect leverage point for someone else. *Your UDL team's epiphany can become another team's stepping stone.* So, share your UDL journey. Select one or more of the following ideas:

- Keep a journal to capture your UDL team's story.
- Develop a blog to connect with others.
- Produce videos of your UDL practices in action.
- Submit an article to spread the word.
- Create a website to share resources and ideas.
- Write a book to memorialize your UDL journey.

UDL as Positive Disruption

When David Rose retired from CAST in 2017, he observed that "the field of UDL is now happily populated by a powerful and inspiring group of new leaders—teachers, researchers, administrators, developers—who are both eager and capable of guiding the next steps along the upward journey, both in the USA and worldwide" (Rose, 2017). He called on each of us to continue this journey of learning, reminding us that from its inception, UDL was meant to be a force to disrupt inequities in education.

Closer to a marathon than a sprint, this is the work of UDL implementation. It takes commitment, iterative thinking, and steady persistence to move the work forward. When our data look positive, we must dig deeper, carefully examining the data to identify the learner variability that is not being addressed. We know that our classrooms are becoming more diverse each day. As UDL implementers, we must ask ourselves what it means to create culturally responsive, universally designed learning environments that address the variability that sits before us. We recognize that our students come to us with varied ways of engaging with one another, accessing content, and demonstrating learning. These differences must impact how we design our learning environments, especially in traditional settings that were never designed with variability in mind.

Rather than viewing UDL as an ultimate destination, David Rose (2017) compared UDL implementation to a journey "worth doing." As you move forward, your unique UDL experiences will build a system that has a deep understanding of how to create expert learners across a spectrum of learner variability. We are convinced that this is work *worth doing* and that the resources in this book will help you along the way.

Your UDL journey awaits!

> *Success is a journey, not a destination. It requires constant effort, vigilance and reevaluation.*
>
> —MARK TWAIN, American author

Resources

This section includes resources developed during the UDL Professional Development System (UDL-PDS) project funded by the Bill and Melinda Gates Foundation and CAST.

CONTENTS

- UDL Knowledge, Beliefs, and Practice survey
- UDL Implementation Willingness and Interest survey
- UDL Professional Development Needs Assessment survey

NOTE You are free to copy and utilize these resources but please be sure to maintain the CAST copyright statement.

UDL KNOWLEDGE, BELIEFS, AND PRACTICE SURVEY

Belief

1. I believe that all learners can learn in general education settings.

LEVEL OF AGREEMENT

Am not sure at this time	Strongly disagree	Somewhat disagree	Agree	Somewhat agree	Strongly agree

2. I believe that there is a range of learning variability in learners in any education setting.

LEVEL OF AGREEMENT

Am not sure at this time	Strongly disagree	Somewhat disagree	Agree	Somewhat agree	Strongly agree

3. I believe learning occurs as a dynamic interaction between the individual and the environment.

LEVEL OF AGREEMENT

Am not sure at this time	Strongly disagree	Somewhat disagree	Agree	Somewhat agree	Strongly agree

4. I believe that the implementation of UDL will lead to better achievement for all learners.

LEVEL OF AGREEMENT

Am not sure at this time	Strongly disagree	Somewhat disagree	Agree	Somewhat agree	Strongly agree

5. I believe UDL implementation can occur with or without technology.

LEVEL OF AGREEMENT

Am not sure at this time	Strongly disagree	Somewhat disagree	Agree	Somewhat agree	Strongly agree

Belief and Practice

1. I believe goals should not include the means by which mastery can be attained and demonstrated.

LEVEL OF AGREEMENT

Am not sure at this time	Strongly disagree	Somewhat disagree	Agree	Somewhat agree	Strongly agree

Please provide examples of ways in which you design/write instruction and assessment goals that do not include means:

_____

_____

2. I believe all learners can benefit from having multiple curricular options or learning pathways.

LEVEL OF AGREEMENT

Am not sure at this time	Strongly disagree	Somewhat disagree	Agree	Somewhat agree	Strongly agree

3. I believe curricular methods and materials should recruit and sustain learner engagement in learning.

LEVEL OF AGREEMENT

Am not sure at this time	Strongly disagree	Somewhat disagree	Agree	Somewhat agree	Strongly agree

4. I provide multiple curriculum options for the benefit of all learners using the following practices:

_____

_____

5. I believe assessment, methods, and materials should be clearly aligned with the curriculum goals.

LEVEL OF AGREEMENT

Am not sure at this time	Strongly disagree	Somewhat disagree	Agree	Somewhat agree	Strongly agree

6. I believe assessments should remove or reduce barriers for more accurate measurement of learner knowledge, skills, and engagement.

LEVEL OF AGREEMENT

Am not sure at this time	Strongly disagree	Somewhat disagree	Agree	Somewhat agree	Strongly agree

Provide examples of how you align curriculum goals with assessment, teaching methods, and materials:

_____

_____

7. I believe supports and scaffolds available during instruction and practice should also be available during assessment when not related to the construct being measured.

LEVEL OF AGREEMENT

I do not plan to do this.	I am willing to learn more about how to do this.	**I plan** to do this.	**I occasionally** (≤33%) do this.	I do this **some** of the time (34–66).	I do this **most** of the time (67–100%).

8. To obtain the most accurate measures of my learners, I remove or reduce barriers by

_____

_____

9. In my classroom instruction, practice, and assessment, I provide the following types of construct irrelevant supports and scaffolds:

_____

_____

10. I work to gain and maintain learner engagement using the following practice(s):

_____

_____

Knowledge and Practice

1. Learners should be provided with a variety of ways for recruiting and sustaining engagement in the instructional environment.

LEVEL OF AGREEMENT

I don't know what this is.	I have heard of this before, but I am not sure how to do this.	I have some knowledge about how to do this but don't feel I am competent.	I am probably competent in my current knowledge of how to do this and would like to learn more.	I am quite competent in my current knowledge of how to do this.	I am very knowledgeable about how to do this and feel competent in my ability to teach others.

2. Learners should be provided with strategies for personal coping skills, self-assessment, and reflection in support of self-regulation.

LEVEL OF KNOWLEDGE

I don't know what this is.	I have heard of this before, but I am not sure how to do this.	I have some knowledge about how to do this but don't feel I am competent.	I am probably competent in my current knowledge of how to do this and would like to learn more.	I am quite competent in my current knowledge of how to do this.	I am very knowledgeable about how to do this and feel competent in my ability to teach others.

3. I provide options for recruiting and sustaining learner engagement by

_____

_____

4. Learners should be provided with multiple ways to access information including text, oral presentation, and visuals.

LEVEL OF KNOWLEDGE

I don't know what this is.	I have heard of this before, but I am not sure how to do this.	I have some knowledge about how to do this but don't feel I am competent.	I am probably competent in my current knowledge of how to do this and would like to learn more.	I am quite competent in my current knowledge of how to do this.	I am very knowledgeable about how to do this and feel competent in my ability to teach others.

5. I provide strategies for personal coping skills, self-assessment, and reflection in support of self-regulation by

_____

_____

Your UDL Journey

6. Varied strategies for a range of learners should be provided to support comprehension/understanding.

LEVEL OF KNOWLEDGE

I don't know what this is.	I have heard of this before, but I am not sure how to do this.	I have some knowledge about how to do this but don't feel I am competent.	I am probably competent in my current knowledge of how to do this and would like to learn more.	I am quite competent in my current knowledge of how to do this.	I am very knowledgeable about how to do this and feel competent in my ability to teach others.

7. I provide multiple ways to present instructional materials/information by

_____

_____

8. Learners should be provided with options for action, expression, and communication during instruction/teaching.

LEVEL OF KNOWLEDGE

I don't know what this is.	I have heard of this before, but I am not sure how to do this.	I have some knowledge about how to do this but don't feel I am competent.	I am probably competent in my current knowledge of how to do this and would like to learn more.	I am quite competent in my current knowledge of how to do this.	I am very knowledgeable about how to do this and feel competent in my ability to teach others.

9. Learners should be provided with options that support goal setting, strategy development, and progress monitoring.

LEVEL OF KNOWLEDGE

I don't know what this is.	I have heard of this before, but I am not sure how to do this.	I have some knowledge about how to do this but don't feel I am competent.	I am probably competent in my current knowledge of how to do this and would like to learn more.	I am quite competent in my current knowledge of how to do this.	I am very knowledgeable about how to do this and feel competent in my ability to teach others.

10. I provide varied strategies to support comprehension/understanding by

_____

_____

11. I provide options for action, expression, and communication by

_____

_____

12. I provide options that support goal setting, strategy development, and progress monitoring among the learners by

_____

_____

© CAST (2020)

UDL IMPLEMENTATION WILLINGNESS AND INTEREST SURVEY

The following questions assess willingness to engage in transformational change and interest in improving practice. They can serve as a starting point for your system to determine interest in implementing UDL as an instructional and decision-making framework. A Likert scale could be used to facilitate agree/disagree responses to these questions.

The following categories represent components of "interest."

Knowledge

- What is our level of understanding of the elements of UDL?

Skills

- We have the skills necessary to implement UDL.

Values

- The elements of UDL are consistent with the way we think learners should learn.

Resources

- Our system has the resources available to implement UDL.

Effectiveness

- We believe UDL will be an effective means of addressing the needs we have identified.

General questions for determining interest in implementing UDL:

- What is our most critical need?
- What would we like to see done about this need?
- How could UDL be an effective means of addressing our identified needs?
- Are we prepared to justify UDL as our preferred instructional and curricular framework?
- What benefits and risks related to implementing UDL should be considered?
- Are we ready to confront any defined risks?

© CAST (2020)

UDL PROFESSIONAL DEVELOPMENT NEEDS ASSESSMENT SURVEY

The following survey was first developed by Bartholomew Consolidation School Corporation (BCSC) in Columbus, Indiana, as a learning tool for teachers to self-assess their professional learning needs in the area of UDL. Instead of a rating or score, survey participants were provided with feedback based upon each of their answers. The original survey was adapted by CAST during the Gates UDL-PDS project with permission.

For the first two questions, think about a specific lesson.

1. If you polled your learners on whether they could articulate the overall goal of the present lesson,

    Select one of these answers:

    a. A few of the learners would be able to articulate the overall goal of the lesson.

    b. Some learners would be able to articulate the overall goal of the lesson.

    c. Every learner would be able to articulate the overall goal of the lesson.

    d. None of your learners would be able to articulate the overall goal.

FEEDBACK

Congratulations if you answered that every learner could articulate the overall lesson goal.

If you answered that none, few, or some would be able to articulate the overall goal of the lesson, consider this:

The primary purpose behind learners articulating the goal of the lesson is ownership and focus. When learners can articulate what they are doing, they have a greater connection to the responsibility of participating. As educators, we always want our learners to be able to clearly articulate the purpose behind what is being taught. Also, learners should be invited to articulate the goal in whatever way works best for them. This could be verbal recitation, but it could also be pictures, pantomime, music, or any other way they choose. Regardless, all of your learners should always be able to articulate the overall goal of every lesson.

2. If you polled your learners asking them to state their personal learning objectives for the lesson,

Select one of these answers:

   a. All of your learners would clearly state their personal learning objectives.

   b. Some of your learners would clearly state their personal learning objectives.

   c. A few of your learners would clearly state their personal learning objectives.

   d. None of the learners would know their personal learning objectives, or they would all have an identical learning objective.

FEEDBACK

Congratulations if you answered that all of your learners can articulate their personal learning objectives. Do you see that your learners are empowered by knowing their personal learning objectives?

If you answered that none, a few, or some of your learners would clearly state their personal learning objectives for the lesson, consider this:

It is extremely important that each learner understand his or her personal learning objective.

By describing what the learner will be able to do as a result of learning activities, methods, or strategies, the learner individualizes the goal of the lesson. This builds personal relevancy.

For the remaining questions, think about a unit you teach (a unit being a group of lessons focused on teaching specific standards or other goals).

3. In what ways (based on learner variability) do you offer examples of concepts?

   Select one of these answers:
   - **a.** I offer a few types of examples to describe the concept.
   - **b.** I offer multiple (four or more) types of examples to describe the concept.
   - **c.** I offer some types of examples to describe the concept.
   - **d.** I offer one type or example to describe the concept.

FEEDBACK

Congratulations if you answered that you offer multiple types of examples. You are a step closer to meeting the needs of all of your learners.

If you answered that you offer one, a few, or some types of examples to describe the concept consider this:

Learning is different for every learner and every learning environment and is facilitated when learners can make connections between new concepts and known concepts. Knowing the learning strengths of your learners will help you in the design of effective lessons. However, proactively planning for learner variability using the UDL guidelines will help you meet the needs of all your learners.

4. In what ways do you offer examples of the skills to be learned during your unit?

Select one of these answers:
- **a.** I don't offer examples of the skills to be learned.
- **b.** I offer one example to describe the skill to be learned.
- **c.** I offer a few types of examples to describe the skill to be learned.
- **d.** I offer multiple (four or more) types of examples to describe the skill to be learned.

FEEDBACK

Congratulations if you answered that you offer multiple types of examples. You are a step closer to meeting the needs of all of your learners. Providing multiple examples to describe a single skill will make your lesson more accessible and meaningful. Make sure your examples fit with the learning needs (learner variability) of the learners.

By limiting the number of examples you offer to your learners, you limit the chances that they will all understand the new skill. Consider this:

You can offer a limited number of examples if you weave together different types of examples that explain one skill. To fully implement UDL, you need to offer multiple examples that represent the skill that learners need to learn.

5. What amount of reading resources do you use, how do they vary, and are they accessible?

Select one of these answers:
- **a.** I use one resource (e.g., textbook).
- **b.** I locate one or two resources with varying reading levels.
- **c.** I locate two or three resources with varying reading levels including websites.
- **d.** I locate four or five resources with varying reading levels including accessible videos, websites, books, and/or other digital and audio materials.

FEEDBACK

Traditionally, teachers believe the number of and type of instructional resources to be driven by state standards, but this is not true. The standards guide what needs to be taught, not how or what resources should be used. In only a few cases do the standards guide the resources you can use, and those cases related to the use of specific books. Additional content resources can and should be used to support the learners during the lesson. Even if the topic is limited or narrow, it is important to locate more than a few content resources to support learning. When implementing a lesson, learners should have access to multiple resources with varying levels of difficulty so they can access the information they require in a way that matches their skills and needs.

If their access to technology is limited, teachers may feel they are limited to only one or two different kinds of resources. However, additional low-tech options can include trade books (e.g., from a library) that are high interest/low ability. Other options that are relatively low-tech include books on tape or CD. Though technology offers flexibility, its absence cannot be a reason to provide limited resources. Ultimately, you want to locate four or five resources with varying reading levels including accessible videos, websites, books and/or other digital and audio materials.

6. How would you describe other resources you use to provide different levels of challenge?

Select one of these answers:

    a. I use a single resource.

    b. I offer a few resources with a range of difficulty.

    c. I offer some resources with a range of difficulty.

    d. I work with the learners to identify multiple resources with a range of difficulty levels.

FEEDBACK

Congratulations if you replied that you offer multiple resources with a range of difficulty levels.

Offering a few or some resources that range in difficulty expands the possibility that your learners will be engaged and that the information is represented in a way that is meaningful. This choice, however, is still limiting to a number of learners in your classroom in two ways. First, resources cannot represent the varying range of difficulty demonstrated in most classrooms. Second, the learners weren't involved in the process. Learners who are more involved in the learning process, which includes the selection of materials, are more engaged and responsive to the lesson overall. Including learners in the selection of the materials pulls them into a decision-making process that builds a sense of ownership. Learners who have ownership of a lesson are more likely to focus on it.

When you only use a single source, you limit the number of learners who will be able to access or learn the information. Brain research tells us that we each process information differently, so to only provide access to one text guarantees the disengagement of some learners. Gaining input from learners on which resources they find most helpful will better ensure your ability to meet their learning needs. Resources can include websites, videos, books, tapes, calculators, or any other device or object that assists learners with understanding a topic. Working with your learners to identify multiple resources with a range of difficulty levels would demonstrate your full understanding and application of the principles of UDL.

7. How have you utilized the learners' background knowledge for the unit?

Select one of these answers:

   a. I identified background knowledge, assessed learner knowledge, and worked with learners to identify meaningful and relevant examples of concepts and skills in real world situations.

   b. I identified background knowledge and assessed learners' knowledge at the beginning of the unit.

   c. I identified what background knowledge was needed for the unit.

   d. I did not assess learners' prior knowledge at the beginning of the unit.

FEEDBACK

Congratulations if you answered that you identified background knowledge, assessed learner prior knowledge, and worked with your learners to identify meaningful and relevant examples.

Prior knowledge is the basis of all learning. If you do not have a clear understanding of your learners' prior knowledge of a topic, you don't know where to begin your lesson. The guidelines of UDL suggest assessing your learners' background knowledge, partnering with your learners to identify real world and relevant examples, and assisting your learners in choosing appropriate levels of reading materials.

8. In what ways were learners able to demonstrate their knowledge or skill?

Select one of these answers:

   a. Learners chose best or preferred types of working situations (e.g., individual vs. group) and varied approaches and means to demonstrate their knowledge or skills.

   b. Learners were offered one way to demonstrate their knowledge or skills.

   c. Learners were offered varied approaches to demonstrate their knowledge or skills.

   d. Learners chose different means to demonstrate their knowledge or skills.

FEEDBACK

Congratulations if you responded that your learners were able to choose the best working situation (e.g., individual vs. group) and approach for each of them to successfully demonstrate their knowledge or skills.

When applying UDL, the principle of expression is frequently addressed through assessment. It is extremely important that teachers provide learners with multiple ways to demonstrate their understanding of information. Providing four or five approaches for expression is a solid step toward applying the UDL principle of expression. Finding the approaches that are the best fit for each learner helps them to understand their own expressive strengths.

By limiting learners to a single approach to demonstrate their knowledge, you are not truly assessing their knowledge. All teachers should strive to provide learners with multiple assessment and expression options over time so the learners can understand which options work best for them.

9. Overall, what kind of support was offered during times of independent practice?

   Select one of these answers:
   - **a.** No learner support was provided.
   - **b.** Support was offered through checking and prompting by the teacher.
   - **c.** Support was offered through checking and prompting, and occasional paired or group work was provided.
   - **d.** Support was offered through checking and prompting, and paired or group work was provided on a regular basis.

FEEDBACK

Congratulations if you answered that support and prompting was offered and paired or group work was provided on a regular basis.

Many of us were taught that independent practice is narrowly defined as the learner working alone, silently, thereby proving he or she knows the information. UDL challenges this assumption by helping us understand that individuals rarely work in seclusion in today's world. Learners need to be able to collaborate to enrich their own learning. Teachers should provide supports through checking and prompting but should also orchestrate regular paired or group work. This paired or group work needs to be structured to report the efforts and outcomes of individuals. By orchestrating regular paired or group work, you can increase learner engagement, provide more opportunities for representation, and gain additional opportunities for expression.

10. How were learners offered support or scaffolds when expressing what they've learned?

    Select one of these answers:

    a. No learner support was provided.

    b. Support was offered through scaffolds and prompting by the teacher.

    c. Support was offered through scaffolds, prompting, and occasional paired or group work.

    d. Support was offered through scaffolds, prompting, and paired or group work on a regular basis.

FEEDBACK

Congratulations if you responded that support was offered through scaffolds, prompting, and paired or group work on a regular basis. Providing learners with a variety of opportunities to demonstrate what they have learned is an important step to providing multiple means of expression. When expressing what they've learned, learners who select from a variety of scaffolds utilize choice and apply knowledge of their own learning strengths.

When learners are given only one opportunity to demonstrate what they've learned (e.g., end of unit exam), their ability to communicate their knowledge is limited by the construct of the assessment tool. The goal of providing multiple options for expression under UDL is to find out what a learner knows, not to find out whether a learner can successfully utilize a specific assessment tool.

References

Aguilar, E. (2016). The art of coaching teams: Building resilient communities that transform schools. San Francisco: Jossey-Bass.

Atkins, M. (2013, October 8). 50 first strength based questions. Strategies approaches and supports, strengths based. [blog] Retrieved from *https://www.changedlives newjourneys.com/50-first-strength-based-questions/*

Bartholomew Consolidated School Corporation (BCSC). (2009). UDL: A framework for BCSC initiatives. [Presentation]. Retrieved from *http://www.bcsc.k12.in.us//site /default.aspx?PageID=349*

Beninghof, A. (2014). Caffeinated learning: How to design and conduct rich, robust professional training. Retrieved from *www.IdeasForEducators.com*

Betts, F. (1992). How systems thinking applies to education. *Educational Leadership, 50*(3), 38–41.

Berquist, E., (Ed.) (2017). UDL: Moving from exploration to integration. Wakefield, MA: CAST Professional Publishing.

Burke, W. (2017). Universal design for learning: Building learner-centered environments in a large district. In E. Berquist (Ed.), *UDL: Moving from exploration to integration* (159–173). Wakefield, MA: CAST Professional Publishing.

Burnes, B. (2004). Kurt Lewin and complexity theories: back to the future? *Journal of Change Management, 4*(4), 309–325.

Cambridge, D., Kaplan, S., & Suter, V. (2005). *Communities of practice design guide: A step-by-step guide for designing & cultivating communities of practice in higher education.* Retrieved from EDUCAUSE *https://library.educause.edu/resources/2005/1/community -of-practice-design-guide-a-stepbystep-guide-for-designing-cultivating-communities-of -practice-in-higher-education*

Cashman, J., Linehan, P., Purcell, L., Rosser, M., Schultz, S., & Skalski, S. (2014). *Leading by convening: A blueprint for authentic engagement.* Alexandria, VA: National Association of State Directors of Special Education.

Cashman, J., Linehan, P., & Rosser, M. (2007). *Communities of Practice: A new approach to solving complex educational problems.* Alexandria, VA: National Association of State Directors of Special Education.

CAST. (2012). *UDL implementation strategy guide.* Wakefield, MA: Author.

CAST. (2014). *UDL Guidelines.* Wakefield, MA: Author.

CAST. (2016, February 17). UDL in the ESSA. Retrieved from *http://www.cast.org/whats-new/news/2016/udl-in-the-essa.html#.XJEFQvZFwmJ*

CAST & the Danielson Framework. (2014). *Crosswalk between Universal Design for Learning (UDL) and the Danielson Framework for Teaching (FfT).* Retrieved from *https://www.k12.wa.us/sites/default/files/public/tpep/frameworks/danielson/danielson_udl_crosswalk.pdf*

Center for Advanced Research on Language Acquisition (2009). *What is culture?* Minneapolis: University of Minnesota. Retrieved from *http://carla.umn.edu/culture/definitions.html.*

Center on Technology and Disability (n.d.) *District spotlight: Bartholomew Consolidated School Corporation, Columbus, Indiana.* Retrieved from *https://cosn.org/sites/default/files/BCSC-DistrictSpotlight-508.pdf*

City, E. A., Elmore, R. F., Fiarman, S. E., & Teitel, L. (2009). *Instructional rounds in education: A network approach to improving teaching and learning.* Cambridge, MA: Harvard Education Press.

Cohen, J. (2014). School climate policy and practice trends: A paradox. A commentary. *Teachers College Record.* Retrieved from *https://www.schoolclimate.org/themes/schoolclimate/assets/pdf/policy/SCPolicy&PracticeTrends-CommentaryTCRecord2-28-14.pdf*

Collins, J. (2001). *Good to great: Why some companies make the leap . . . and others don't.* New York: HarperCollins Publishers, Inc.

Conzemius, A., & O'Neill, J. (2002). *The handbook for SMART school teams.* Bloomington, IN: National Educational Service.

Darling-Hammond, L., Hyler, M., Gardner, M. (2017). *Effective teacher professional development.* Palo Alto, CA: Learning Policy Institute.

Datnow, A. (2011). Collaboration and contrived collegiality: Revisiting Hargreaves in the age of accountability. *Journal of Educational Change, 12*(2), 147–158.

Deutschman, A. (2007). *Change or die: Could you change when change matters most?* New York: HarperCollins Publishers, Inc.

Doran, G. T. (1981). There's a S.M.A.R.T. way to write management's goals and objectives. *Management Review, 70*(11), 35–36.

Dreyfus, H., & Dreyfus, S. (1986). *Mind over machine.* New York: Free Press.

DuFour, R., DuFour, R., Eaker, R. & Many, T. (2006). *Learning by doing: A handbook for professional communities at work.* Bloomington, IN: Solution Tree.

Fixsen, D. L., Blase, K. A., Horner, R., & Sugai, G. (2009, February). *Readiness for change. Scaling up,* Brief #3. Chapel Hill: The University of North Carolina, FPG, SISEP.

Fixsen, D. L., Naoom, S. F., Blasé, K. A., Friedman, R. M., & Wallace, F. (2005). *Implementation research: A synthesis of the literature.* Tampa: University of South Florida, Louis de la Parte Florida Mental Health Institute, NIRN (FMHI Publication #231).

Friend, M., & Cook, L. (1992, March). The new mainstreaming. *Instructor 101*(7), 30–36.

Fullan, M. (1993). *Change Forces: Probing the Depths of Educational Reform.* London: Falmer Press.

Fullan, M. (1999). *Change forces: The sequel.* Philadelphia: Falmer Press.

Fullan, M. (2001). *Leading in a culture of change.* San Francisco: Jossey Bass.

Fullan, M. (2010). *All systems go.* Thousand Oaks, CA: Corwin Press.

Ganley, P. & Ralabate, P. (2013). *UDL implementation: A tale of four districts.* Retrieved from National Center on Universal Design for Learning.

Giotis, T. (2012). *Advancing project stakeholders management by using structured dialogic design (SDD)* Paper presented at PMI® Global Congress 2012—EMEA, Marseilles, France. Newtown Square, PA: Project Management Institute. Retrieved from *https://www.pmi.org/learning/library/advancing-project-stakeholders-management-using-sdd-6424*

Guskey, T. R. (2000). *Evaluating professional development.* Thousand Oaks, CA: Corwin Press.

Guskey, T. R. (2002). Professional development and teacher change. *Teachers and teaching: Theory and practice, 8*(3/4), 381–391.

Hackman, J. R. (2002). A real team. In J. R. Hackman (Ed.), *Leading teams: Setting the stage for great performances,* 37–60. Boston: Harvard Business School Press.

Hall, G. E., & Hord, S. M. (2001). *Implementing change: Patterns, principles and potholes.* Needham Heights, MA: Allyn and Bacon.

Hall, P. & Simeral, A. (2008). *Building teachers' capacity for success. A collaborative approach for coaches and school leaders.* Alexandria, VA: Association for Supervision and Curriculum Development.

Hargreaves, A. (1994). Collaboration and contrived collegiality: Cup of comfort or poisoned chalice? In Hargreaves, A. *Changing teachers, changing times,* 186–221. New York: Teachers College Press.

Hargreaves A., & Fink D. (2009). Distributed leadership: Democracy or delivery? In: Harris A. (eds.) *Distributed leadership: Different perspectives.* Studies in Educational Leadership (7). New York: Springer.

Hargreaves, A. & Shirley, D. (2009). *The fourth way: The inspiring future for educational change.* Thousand Oaks, CA: Corwin Press.

Hargreaves, M. (2010). *Evaluating Systems Change: A Planning Guide.* Princeton, NJ: Mathematica Policy Research, Inc.

Hidalgo, N. (1993). Multicultural teacher introspection. In Perry, T. and Fraser, J. (Eds.) *Freedom's plow: Teaching in the multicultural classroom.* New York: Routledge.

Hord, S. M. (1997). *Professional Learning Communities: Communities of continuous inquiry and improvement.* Retrieved from *http://www.sedl.org/pubs/change34/*

Hunzicker, J. (2004). The beliefs-behavior connection: Leading teachers toward change. *Principal, 84*(2), 44–46.

IDEA Partnership. (2007, February) *Communities of practice: A new approach to solving complex educational problems.* Alexandria, VA: National Association of State Directors of Special Education. Retrieved from *http://www.ideapartnership.org/documents/CoPGuide.pdf.*

IDEO (2013). Design Thinking for Educators Toolkit. Cambridge, MA: IDEO. *https://designthinkingforeducators.com/*

Kaye, G. and Resnick, I. (1994). *Climate diagnostic tool: The six R's of participation.* Brooklyn, NY: Community Development Consultants.

Killion, J., Roy, P, & von Frank, V. (2009). *Becoming a learning school.* Oxford, OH: National Staff Development Council (Learning Forward).

Kim, D. H. (2001). *Organizing for learning: Strategies for knowledge creation and enduring change.* Waltham, MA: Pegasus Communications.

Kim, K. H., & Cory, D. (2008). *It begins here: Learning partners toolkit.* Battle Creek, MI: W. K. Kellogg Foundation.

Kippenberger, T. (1998). Planned change: Kurt Lewin's legacy. *The Antidote, 3*(4), 10–12.

Latham, N. (2014). *A practical guide to evaluating systems change in a human services system context.* Washington, DC: Center for Evaluation Innovation. Retrieved from *http://www.evaluationinnovation.org/publications/practical-guide-evaluating-systems-change-human-services-system-context*

Lave, J. & Wenger, E. (1991). *Situated learning: Legitimate peripheral participation.* Cambridge, UK: Cambridge University Press.

Lavoie, R. (1989). *How difficult can this be? The F.A.T. City workshop.* Alexandria, VA: PBS Video.

Leverenz, C. S. (2014). Design thinking and the wicked problem of teaching writing. *ScienceDirect.* Retrieved from *www.sciencedirect.com.*

Lewin, K. (1958) Group decisions and social change. In T. M. Newcomb and E. L. Hartley (Eds.) *Reading in social psychology* (197–211). New York: Henry Holt.

Little, J. W. (1982). Norms of collegiality and experimentation: Workplace conditions of school success. *American Educational Research Journal, 19*(3), 325–340.

MacDonald, E. B. (2013). *The skillful team leader.* Thousand Oaks, CA: Corwin & Learning Forward.

Marzano, R. J. (2003). *What works in schools: Translating research into action.* Alexandria, VA: ASCD.

Mattatall, C. & Power, K. (2018). Teacher collaboration and achievement of students with LDs: A review of the research. *LD@School.* Retrieved from *https://www.ldatschool.ca/the-impact-of-teacher-collaboration-on-academic-achievement-and-social-development-for-student-with-learning-disabilities-a-review-of-the-research/*

McGoff, C. (2012). *The PRIMES: How any group can solve any problem.* Hoboken, NJ: John Wiley & Sons. Retrieved from *http://www.theprimes.com/change-vs-transformation*

McLeskey, J, & Waldron, N. (2002). School change and inclusive schools: Lessons learned from practice. *Phi Delta Kappan, 84*(1).

Meyer, A., Rose, D. H., & Gordon, D. (2014). *Universal Design for Learning: Theory and practice.* Wakefield, MA: CAST Professional Publishing.

Minow, M. L. (2009) Designing learning for all learners. In D. T. Gordon, J. W. Gravel, & L. A. Schifter (Eds.). *A policy reader in Universal Design for Learning* (ix-xiv) Cambridge, MA: Harvard Education Press.

National Center on Universal Design for Learning. (2012). *UDL implementation: A process of change* [Online seminar presentation & transcript]. UDL Series, no. 3.

National Center on Universal Design for Learning. (2014). *UDL and expert learners.* Retrieved from *http://www.udlcenter.org/aboutudl/expertlearner*

National Center on Universal Design for Learning. (2017). *UDL guidelines—Theory & practice.* Retrieved from *http://www.udlcenter.org/aboutudl/udlguidelines*

National Center on Secondary Education and Transition (NCSET). (2005). *Essential tools, Improving secondary education and transition for youth with disabilities: Community resource mapping.* Minneapolis, MN: University of Minnesota. Author. Retrieved from *http://www.ncset.org/publications/essentialtools/mapping/NCSET_EssentialTools_ResourceMapping.pdf*

Nelson, L. L. (2014). *Design and deliver: Planning and teaching using Universal Design for Learning.* Baltimore: Paul H. Brookes Publishing.

New England Association of Schools and Colleges (NEASC). (2016). *Guide to developing core values, beliefs, and learning expectations.* Burlington, MA: Author.

New Zealand Ministry of Education. (2017). *Karori Normal School: Implementing UDL across our school.* [Online Vimeo presentation]. Retrieved from *https://vimeo.com/album/2950799/video/220721010*

Nicol, J. (2014). *Universal design for learning promotes student engagement—An action research project at Island View School.* Retrieved from *https://www.theudlproject.com*

Novak, K. (2016). *UDL now! A teacher's guide to implementing Universal Design for Learning in today's classrooms.* Wakefield, MA: CAST Professional Publishing.

Novak, K. & Rodriguez, K. (2016). *Universally designed leadership: Applying UDL to systems and schools.* Wakefield, MA: CAST Professional Publishing.

Novick, B., Kress, J. S., & Elias, M. (2002) *Building learning communities with character.* Alexandria, VA: ASCD.

Nussbaum-Beach, S. & Ritter Hall, L. (2012). *The connected educator: Learning and leading in the digital age.* Bloomington, IN: Solution Tree Press.

Partnership for 21st Century Learning. (2009). *Framework for 21st century learning.* Retrieved from *http://www.battelleforkids.org/networks/p21*

Patton, M. Q. & Patrizi, P. A. (2010). Strategy as the focus for evaluation. In P. A. Patrizi & M. Q. Patton (Eds.), Evaluating strategy [Special issue]. *New Directions for Evaluation,* 128, 5–28.

Payne, R. K. (1995). *A framework for understanding and working with students and adults from poverty.* Baytown, TX: RFT.

Quick, J. (2012, February 7). *Bartholomew Consolidated School Corporation: An overview of one system's implementation of Universal Design for Learning and the use of accessible technology to improve the learning of all students.* Retrieved from *https://www.help.senate.gov/imo/media/doc/Quick.pdf*

Ragland, M. A., Clubine, B., Constable, D., & Smith, P. A. (2002). *Expecting success: A study of five high performing, high poverty schools.* Washington, DC: Council of Chief State School Officers.

Ralabate, P. K. (2016). *Your UDL lesson planner: The step-by-step guide for teaching all learners.* Baltimore: Paul H. Brookes Publishing.

Ralabate, P., Hehir, T., Grindal, T., Eidelman, H., Dodd, E., Vue, G., Karger, J., Smith, F., & Carlisle, A. (2012). *Understanding the impact of the Race to the Top and ARRA funding on the promotion of Universal Design for Learning.* Wakefield, MA: National Center on UDL.

Ralabate, P. K., & Nelson, L. L. (2017). *Culturally responsive design for English learners: The UDL approach.* Wakefield, MA: CAST Publishing.

Rao, K., & Berquist, E. (2017). A co-teaching conversation: Using UDL to co-plan for the inclusive classroom. In E. Berquist (Ed.), *UDL: Moving from exploration to integration.* (pp. 121–138). Wakefield, MA: CAST Professional Publishing.

Rao, K., Currie-Rubin, R., & Logli, C. (2016). *UDL and inclusive practices in IB schools worldwide.* Wakefield, MA: CAST Professional Learning.

Rappolt-Schlichtmann, G., Daley, S. G., & Rose, L. T., Eds. (2012). *A research reader in Universal Design for Learning.* Cambridge, MA: Harvard Education Press.

Reeves, D. B. (2009). *Leading change in your school: How to conquer myths, build commitment, and get results.* Alexandria, VA: ASCD.

Richardson, V. (1998). How teachers change: What will lead to change that most benefits student learning? *Focus on Basics, 2*(C). NCSALL: National Center for the Study of Adult Learning and Literacy.

Rinehart, T. A., Laszlo, A. T., & Briscoe, G. O. (2001). *Collaboration toolkit: How to build, fix, and sustain productive partnerships.* Washington, DC: US Department of Justice, Office of Community Oriented Policing Services.

Rose, D. (2017). A message from David Rose. Retrieved from *http://www.cast.org/whats-new/news/2017/a-message-from-david-rose.html*

Rose, L. T., Rouhani, P., & Fischer, K. W. (2013). The science of the individual. *Mind, Brain, and Education, 7*(3), 152–158.

Rose, T. (2016). *The end of average: Unlocking our potential by embracing what makes us different.* New York: HarperCollins Publisher.

Rowling, J. K. (2007). *Harry Potter and the deathly hallows.* London: Bloomsbury Publishing.

RTI Action Network. (n.d.). *What is RTI?* Retrieved from *http://www.rtinetwork.org/learn/what/whatisrti*

Sadera, W., & Hargrave, C. (2005). Conceptual change in pre-service teacher technology preparation. In C. Vrasidas & G. V. Glass (Eds.), *Preparing teachers to teach with technology.* (pp. 291–302). Greenwich, CT: Information Age.

Sanchez, R., Berquist, E., & Omelan, K. (2017). Transforming high school learning environments: Our UDL implementation journey at César E. Chávez High School. In E. Berquist (Ed.), *UDL: Moving from exploration to integration.* (pp. 99–119). Wakefield, MA: CAST Professional Publishing.

Sanetti, L. H., Kratochwill, T. R., Volpiansky, P., & Ring, M. (2011). *Resource mapping: A toolkit.* Wisconsin Department of Public Instruction. Retrieved from *http://sss.usf.edu/resources/presentations/2011/FASSW/EOCA%20Wisconsin.pdf*

Santamaria, L. J., & Thousand, J. S. (2004). Collaboration, co-teaching, and differentiated instruction: A process-oriented approach to whole schooling. *International Journal of Whole Schooling, 1*(1), 13–27. Retrieved from *https://eric.ed.gov/?id=EJ854544*

Schalock, M. D. & Fredericks, B. (1994). The house that traces built: A conceptual model of service delivery systems and implications for change. *Journal of Special Education, 28*(2), 203–241.

Senge, P. M. (1990). *The fifth discipline—The art and practice of a learning organization.* New York: Doubleday.

Senge, P., Kleiner, A., Roberts, C., Ross, R., Roth, G., & Smith, B. (1999). *The dance of change: The challenges of sustaining momentum in learning organizations.* New York: Doubleday.

Snow, E., Lynn, J. & Beer, T. (2015). Strategy design amid complexity: Tools for designing and implementing adaptive funding strategies. *The Foundation Review, 7*(2), Article 4. Retrieved from *https://scholarworks.gvsu.edu/tfr/vol7/iss2/4/.*

Sopko, K. (2008). *Universal Design for Learning: Implementation in six local education agencies.* (Project Forum). Alexandria, VA: National Association of State Directors of Special Education.

Stacey, R. D. (1996). *Complexity and creativity in organizations.* San Francisco: Berrett-Koehler Publishers.

Stiggins, R. (2002, June). Assessment crisis: The absence of learning. *Phi Delta Kappan, 83*(10), 758–765.

SWIFT Center. (2016). *Facilitating resource mapping & matching.* Lawrence, KS: Author. Retrieved from *http://www.swiftschools.org/sites/default/files/Facilitating%20 Resource%20Mapping%20%26%20Matching.pdf*

Team BE. (2011, December). *Communities versus teams?* Retrieved from *http://wenger-trayner.com/resources/how-are-communities-of-practice-different-from-more-familiar-structures-like-teams-or-task-forces/*

Thessin, R. A., & Starr, J. P. (2011). Supporting the Growth of Effective Professional Learning Communities Districtwide. *Phi Delta Kappan, 92*(6), 4854.

Turnbull, H. R., Stowe, M. J., & Huerta, N. E. (2007). *Free appropriate public education: The law and children with disabilities.* (7th ed.). Denver, CO: Love Publishing Company.

van Horn, G. (2015). *Bartholomew's elevated path leads through UDL.* AASA Toolbox. Retrieved from *http://my.aasa.org/AASA/Toolbox/SAMag/Nov15/VanHorn.aspx*

Waldron, N. L. & McLeskey, J. (2010). Establishing a collaborative school culture through comprehensive school reform. *Journal of Educational and Psychological Consultation, 20,* 58–74.

Wenger, E. (1998). *Communities of practice: Learning, meaning, and identity.* Cambridge, UK: Cambridge University Press.

Wheelock, A. (2000). Professional collaboration to improve teacher and student work. *Conversations: Turning points, transforming middle schools, (1)*1. Boston: Center for Collaborative Education.

Williamson, R. & Blackburn, B. (2010). *Rigorous schools and classrooms: Leading the Way.* Larchmont, NY: Eye on Education.

Wolff, T. (2002). A practical approach to evaluating coalitions. In T. Backer (Ed.). *Evaluating community collaborations* (57–112). New York: Springer.

Index

NUMBERS
3-2-1 Assessment, using for readiness, 61–62

A
ACCESS (Adapting Curriculum and Classroom Environments for Student Success), 51–53, 65–66
accountability. *See* "Results-Driven Accountability;" shared accountability
action and expression
    aspects of culture, 142–143
    Optimize phase, 149
    principle of, 6
    Scale phase, 134
    UDL CoP, 125
    UDL implementation, 35–36, 44
    willingness and interest, 56
action plan, developing, 82–83, 86. *See also* implementation process
African proverb, 40
Aguilar (2016), 139, 141
Aguilar, Elena, 96
aiming high, 40–41, 70–72
AIMS (Alexis I. DuPont Middle School), 52
Algonquin and Lakeshore Catholic School District Board, Ontario, Canada, 31–33, 61–62
All Systems Go, 12–13
Attainable SMART goal, 78
authenticity, 43
average, myth of, 72
awareness, building, 53, 59–60, 64–65

B
Baltimore County Public Schools, 97–98
BCPS (Baltimore County Public Schools), 89, 156
    Scale phase, 117–119

BCSC (Bartholomew Consolidated School Corporation)
    example, 23–24
    integrate with what exists, 106
    Optimize phase, 137–138, 141, 143–144
    PD needs assessment, 172–181
    predict and plan, 150
    Prepare phase, 68, 73
    Scale phase, 128–129
    system UDL implementation, 157
    UDL and brain networks, 7
    UDL coaching, 103
behavioral aspect of culture, 140
beliefs
    perspectives and values, 9, 21
    practice surveys, 164–167
Beninghof, Anne, 98
Berquist (2017)
    coaching UDL, 103
    debunking myths, 73
    five phases of UDL implementation, 34
    leadership PLCs, 122
    professional learning, 43, 100
    UDL-CoP, 123
    UDL definition, 5
Berquist; New Zealand Ministry of Education; Nicol; Rao et al.; Rappolt-Schlichtmann, Daley, & Rose, 8
Berquist; Rappolt-Schlichtmann, Daley, & Rose, 8
better or improved, 10
Betts, F., 25
BLT (Building Leadership Team), 52–53
book study, UDL-PLCs, 101
bottom-up leadership, 150
brain networks, 6–7
Bright Morning, 96
budget-saving aspects, 59

Burke, Billy, 97–98
Burnes (2004), 150
Burnes; Fullan; Hall & Hord; Kippenberger; Lewin; Schalock & Fredericks; Senge et al.; Stacey, 26
Burnes; Kippenberger; Lewin, 9

C

Cambridge, Kaplan, and Suter, 121
Cashman, Linehan, & Rosser, 93
Cashman et al., 42
CAST (2012), 9, 34
CAST (2016), 5
CAST Research website, 161
Cecil County public schools, 156
César E. Chávez High School, 103, 131
change. *See also* need for change; systems change
    initiatives, 4
    need for, 9, 19
    vs. transformation, 9–12
civil or human rights, linkage to, 59
coaching UDL, 103–104
co-acting group vs. team, 94
coercion vs. collaboration, 91–92
collaboration
    vs. cooperation, 96
    fostering, 42, 108
    gauging, 109–110
    Integrate phase, 90–92
Collins, J., 13
commitment, fostering, 39–40
communication and expression, 44
conferences and symposium, attending, 160
Congress
    ESSA (Every Student Succeeds Act), 5
    Higher Education Opportunity Act of 2008, 5
consensus in shared leadership, 41
continuity and consistency, 10
contrived collegiality
    vs. collaboration, 91–92
    and leadership structures, 150
Conzemius & O'Neill, 78
CoP (community of practice) vs. PLC (professional learning communities), 120–126
core values, 21, 29–30, 39. *See also* values, perspectives, and beliefs
culture, dimensions of, 139–140
current reality, 20–21, 28–29

D

Darling-Hammon, Hyler, and Gardener, 99
DDOE (Delaware Department of Education), 52
de Saint-Exupéry, Antoine, 79, 93
design thinking model, 81–82
Deutschman, A., 10
dialogue protocol, 62–64
Diedrich, Jeff, 55
dieting, 10
Discovery in design thinking, 81
dissatisfaction and need for change, 10–11, 15
Doran, George, 78
DuFour, DuFour, Eaker, & Many, 95

E

early adopters, 54
educator experience, developing, 108
effectiveness, evidence of, 59
effort and persistence, sustaining, 44
Eisenhower, Dwight D., 77
ELs (English learners), funding for, 158
engagement
    aspects of culture, 142–143
    assessing readiness, 54
    Integrate phase, 94
    and readiness, 55
    representation and action, 6, 35
    in shared leadership, 42
    of team, 42
    UDL implementation crosswalk, 44
    UDL-CoP, 124–125
equity in shared leadership, 41
ESEA (Elementary and Secondary Education Act), 5, 105, 158
ESSA (Every Student Succeeds Act), 5
evaluate, infuse, create, 108
Evaluate-Refresh-Recycle stage, resource mapping, 75
evidence leads the way, Scale phase, 132–134
Evolution in design thinking, 82
executive functions, UDL implementation crosswalk, 44
expectations, setting, 40–41, 70–72
experienced vs. novice educators, 127–128
Experimentation in design thinking, 82
expert learning, 72, 160. *See also* learning; professional learning experiences
expertise, building, 159–162

Explore phase
 awareness, 59–60, 64–65
 building awareness, 97
 engagement, 54–55
 investigate, 57, 64
 overview, 36, 53
 readiness, 54–55, 61–62
 recognition, 59
 variability, 57–58
 willingness and interest, 55–56
expression and communication, 44

F

fairness, concept of, 72
Fixsen, Blase, Horner, & Sugai, 54
Fixsen, et al., 34, 150
Fixsen, Naoom, Blase, Friedman, & Wallace, 7
Fixsen et al.; Reeves; Senge et al., 10
flexibility
 as key, 43
 prioritizing, customizing, and infusing, 80
flywheel effect, 12–13
formative evaluation protocols, Scale phase, 133–134
foundation, building, 45–47
Four Ps, 104–106, 113–114
Fullan, Michael, 12–13, 23, 39, 144
Fullan; Marzano; Ragland, Clubine, Constable, & Smith, 39
funding barriers, solutions to, 157–159

G

Ganley & Ralabate, 156–157
Gates, Bill and Melinda, 33, 61, 73, 156
Giotis, T., 62
goal directed UDL initiative, 94–95
goals, setting, 40–41. *See also* learning goals
group commitment, 24. *See also* team
group-think process, 21
growth in shared leadership, 41
Gurria, Jose Angel, 121
Guskey, T.R., 21, 99
Guskey; Hunzicker; Sadera & Hargrave, 21

H

Hackman, J.R., 94
Hall & Hord, 9, 70, 139
Hall & Hord; Hargreaves; Little; Mattatall & Power, 91
Hall & Simeral, 100

Hargreaves, A., 92, 150–151
Harry Potter series, 72
HEA (Higher Education Act), 105
HIAT (High Incidence Accessible Technology), 138, 151
Hidalgo's dimensions of culture, 139–140
Higher Education Opportunity Act of 2008, 5
Hillary, Edmund, 56
horizontal leadership structure, 151
how of learning
 brain networks, 6
 measuring completion, 60
 moving into, 19
 resource mapping, 75
 Scale phase, 135
human or civil rights, linkage to, 59
Hunzicker, J., 21

I

IDEA (Individuals with Disabilities Education Act), 105, 158
ideas
 popularity of, 59
 trying out, 21
Ideation in design thinking, 81
"implementation dips," 39
implementation process. *See also* action plan
 action plan, 77
 addressing mindset, 71–72
 crosswalk, 44
 engagement, representation, and action, 35
 Explore phase, 36, 53–60
 goals, 35–36
 graphic, 35–36
 Integrate phase, 36–37, 90–107
 need for change, 36
 Optimize phase, 36, 38, 138–152
 overview, 33–35
 Prepare phase, 36–37, 69–82
 proactive planning, 39–44
 purpose, 34
 Scale phase, 36, 38, 119–134
 variations, 34
 willingness and interest survey, 171
improved or better, 10
improvement, Optimize phase, 138, 143
incentives, embedding, 42
inputs vs. impact, Scale phase, 133
inquiry-based problem solving, UDL-PLCs, 102

instructional and learning environment design, 5
Integrate phase
    alignment with UDL, 104
    collaboration, 90–92, 108–110
    evaluate, infuse, create, 108
    Four Ps, 104–106, 113–114
    goal directed, 94–95
    interdependent, 94–95
    models, 106–107
    mutually accountable, 94–95
    overview, 37
    PD (professional development), 97–100, 108, 111–112
    PLCs (professional learning communities), 100–103
    policies, 105, 113–114
    practices, 106, 113–114
    procedures, 106, 113–114
    processes, 105–106, 113–114
    recruit vs. select, 92–94
    shared responsibility and resources, 95–96
    UDL coaching, 103–104
    using what exists, 106–107
interdependency, concept of, 95
interest, recruiting, 44
interest and willingness
    determining, 61–62
    importance of, 55–56
international implementation, 8
Interpretation in design thinking, 81
investigative questions, 57–58, 64
involvement vs. participation, 42

J

Japanese proverb, 129
JDL journey, sharing, 161

K

Kaye and Resnick, 92
Kazantzakis, Nikos, 23
Kellbaugh, K., 118
Keller, Helen, 41
Kennedy, John F., 13
Kettering, Charles F., 70
Killion, Roy, & von Frank, 43
Kim, D. H., 143
Kim & Correy, 20–21
knowledge and practice survey, 167–170
Knowledge Matrix Template, 58

L

Latham, N., 133
Lavoie, R., 72
leadership
    as driver in Optimize phase, 150–151
    PLCs (professional learning communities), 122
    sharing, 41–42
    team, 44
learner variability, considering, 18–19, 72
learning. *See also* expert learning; professional learning experiences
    ongoing, 155–157
    why, *what*, and *how* of, 6, 19
learning environment, defined, 70
learning goals, defining, 98–99. *See also* goals
learning organization, Optimize phase, 140–141
lesson study, UDL-PLCs, 101
Lewin, Kurt, 9, 25
logic model, developing for awareness, 60

M

MacDonald (2013)
    addressing negative issues, 141
    data-driven dialogue, 132
    fixed mindset, 71
    SMART goals, 78
Malcolm X, 133
Mapping stage, resource mapping, 75
McGoff, Chris, 11–12
McGrath, Bill, 138, 151
MCPS (Montgomery County Public Schools), 138, 146, 151
Mead, Margaret, 24
Measurable SMART goal, 78
members, recruiting during Scale phase, 127–128
Meyer, Rose, and Gordon, 6
Meyer et al., 12, 40, 70, 72
mindset, addressing in implementation process, 71–72
Minow, M. L., 4
MTSS (multitiered systems of support), 57, 105
mutually accountable, 95
Myers, Lorii, 66
myth of average, 72
myths, debunking, 73

N

National Center on Secondary Education and Transition, 76
National Center on Universal Design for Learning, 8, 34, 55, 72
NEASC (New England Association of Schools and Colleges), 21
need for change, 9, 19, 35–36. *See also* change
needs assessment, conducting, 22, 98–99
negative issues, addressing in Optimize phase, 141
Nhat Hanh, Thich, 60
Norris interview, 3–4
Novak (2014), 70
Novak and Rodriguez, 60
novice vs. experienced educators, 127–128
Novick, Kress, & Elias, 54
NSCC (National School Climate Center), 70

O

OASD (Oconomowoc Area School District)
  overview, 67–68
  integrate with what exists, 107
  resource mapping, 74, 76
  UDL climate, 70–71
  UDL coaching, 103
objectives, setting, 42–43
obstacles
  anticipating, 45
  considering in Optimize phase, 149
  overcoming, 39–44
Optimize phase
  action, expression, engagement, 149
  continuous improvement, 138, 145–147
  iterative benefit analysis, 144–147
  leadership as driver, 150–151
  learning at core, 139–143
  maximizing improvement, 143
  measuring growth and progress, 145–146
  overview, 38, 138
  predict and plan, 147–149
  scenario planning, 148–149, 153
  UDL culture, 139–143

P

Padlet.com, 58, 76
participation
  vs. involvement, 42
  six Rs of, 92–93, 96

Partnership for 21st Century Learning, 70
Patton and Patrizi, 132
Payne, R. I., 43
PBS (positive behavior supports), 57
PD (professional development)
  evaluating, 111–112
  needs assessment survey, 172–181
  overview, 97–100
people-first language, 68
persistence and effort, sustaining, 44
perspectives, values, and beliefs, 9
Petersilia, 11
planning. *See* proactive planning
PLCs (professional learning communities), 100–103, 121–126, 156
Policies in Four Ps, 105, 113–114
Practices in Four Ps, 106, 113–114
predict and plan, Optimize phase, 147–150. *See also* proactive planning
Prepare phase
  action plan, 77, 82–83, 86
  debunking myths, 73
  design thinking, 81–82
  expectations, 70–72
  flexibility, 80
  measuring progress, 81
  overview, 37, 69
  resource mapping, 74–76, 83, 85
  SMART goal, 77–80
  SWOT (strengths, weaknesses, opportunities, threats), 84
  UDL climate, 69–70, 83–84
Principles of UDL, 6
proactive planning, 39–44. *See also* predict and plan
Procedures in Four Ps, 106, 113–114
Processes in Four Ps, 105–106, 113–114
professional learning experiences, sharing, 43–44. *See also* expert learning; learning
progress
  assessing, 42–43
  monitoring and measuring, 81
promoting work, 128

Q

Quick; van Horn, 7

R

Ralabate (2016), 73, 78
Ralabate & Nelson, 158

Rao, Currie-Rubin, & Logli, 5
Rao and Berquist, 95
readiness
   assessing, 53–54, 61–62
   developing, 54–55
   staff survey, 61–62
recognition, aspects of culture, 142–143
recruit vs. select, 92–94
recruiting interest, 44
Reeves (2009), 139
Reeves, Douglas B., 131, 144
relationships are paramount, 43
representation
   engagement and action, 6, 35
   UDL CoP, 125
research opportunities, 160–161
resource mapping, 74–76, 83, 85
resources and responsibility, sharing, 95–96
"Results-Driven Accountability," 158. *See also* shared accountability
Results-oriented SMART goal, 78
Richardson, V., 21
Rinehart, Laszlo, & Briscoe, 92
Rogers, Carl, 22
Rose, David, 161–162
Rose, Rouhani, & Fischer, 141
Rose, Todd, 72
Rs of participation, 92–93, 96
RTI (Response to Intervention), 105–106

S

Sadera and Hargrave, 11
Sanchez, Berquist, & Omelan, 131
Sanchez, Rene, 131–132
Sanetti, Kratochwill, Volpiansky, & Ring, 74
Sanetti et al., 75–76
Scale phase
   action, expression, engagement, 134
   alignment with UDL, 128–129
   collaborative community, 120–121
   CoP (community of practice), 120–126
   engagement guidelines, 124
   evidence leads the way, 132–133
   formative evaluation protocols, 133–134
   inputs vs. impact, 133
   novice vs. experienced, 127–128
   overview, 38, 119–120
   PLCs (professional learning communities), 121–126
   promoting work, 128
   recruiting members, 127
   seed then weed, 129–132
   sphere of influence, 126–127
scenario planning, 148–149, 153
school climate, defined, 70
seed then weed, 129–132
self-regulation, 44
Senge, Peter, 20, 25, 140–141
Shakespeare, William, 55
shared accountability, 95. *See also* "Results-Driven Accountability"
shared vision, defining and clarifying, 39–40
sharing
   leadership, 41
   professional learning experiences, 43–44
   responsibility and resources, 95–96
   UDL journey, 161
six Rs of participation, 92–93, 96
SMART goal, defining, 77–80
Snow, Lynn, and Beer, 148
Solution Tree, 96
special education funds, 158
Specific SMART goal, 78
sphere of influence
   graphical representation, 129
   widening, 126
staff surveys and interviews, 61–62
Stiggins, R., 133–134
Strategic Implementation stage, resource mapping, 75
structured dialogue protocol, 63–64
surveys
   knowledge, beliefs, and practice, 164–170
   PD needs assessment, 172–181
   UDL implementation, 171
   willingness and interest, 171
SWIFT Center, resource-mapping resource, 76
SWOT (strengths, weaknesses, opportunities, threats), 84
symbiotic aspect of culture, 140
symposium and conferences, attending, 160
synergy in shared leadership, 41
systemic barriers, anticipating, 45
systems change, 25–27. *See also* change

T

team. *See also* leadership team
   vs. co-acting group, 94
   current reality, 20–21

engagement, 42
interdependence, 94–95
Team BE, 121
Time-bound SMART goal, 78
Title I Title III funding, 158
top-down leadership, 150
"traditional one-shot" PD, 100
transformation vs. change, 9–12, 25–27
transformative framework, UDL as, 12–13
trust in shared leadership, 41
Turnbull, Stowe, & Huerta, 105
Twain, Mark, 162

U

UD CDS (University of Delaware's Center for Disabilities Studies), 51–53
UDL (Universal Design for Learning)
 alignment with, 104, 128–129
 and brain networks, 6–7
 building expertise, 159–162
 coaching, 103–104
 common elements, 8–9
 debunking myths, 73
 development needs assessment survey, 172–181
 dialogue protocol, 63
 flywheel effect, 12–13
 implementation, 7–10, 21–23
 investigating, 53
 knowledge, beliefs, practice survey, 164–170
 as lens, 33–34
 modeling in practice, 43
 mutually accountable, 94–95
 Norris interview, 3–4
 overview, 5–6
 as positive disruption, 161–162
 principles, 6
 and process of change, 4
 research opportunities, 160–161
 resources, 7, 60
 structured dialogue protocol, 63–64
 as transformative framework, 12–13
 use of guidelines, 4
UDL chats, engaging in, 160
UDL climate
 assessing, 83
 creating, 69–70
 SWOT analysis, 84
UDL culture, nurturing, 139–143, 151–152
UDL framework, crosswalk with aspects of culture, 142–143
UDL Implementation and Research Network, 42
UDL-CoP, 120–126
UDL-IRN (UDL Implementation and Research Network), 55, 161
UDL-PLCs, 100–103, 121–126, 156

V

values, perspectives, and beliefs, 9, 23–24. *See also* core values
van Horn, George, 137, 141
variability, respecting, 57–59, 72
views, exchanging, 42
vision, defining and sharing, 39–40
vision statements, examples, 77
von Horn, George, 137

W

webinars, 160
what of learning
 building awareness, 59
 moving beyond, 19
 Principle of Representation, 6
 resource mapping, 75
 Scale phase, 135
where of learning, resource mapping, 75
who and why
 building awareness, 59
 starting with, 20–25, 44
Who of action plan, Scale phase, 135
Who stage, mapping resources, 75
why and how, moving into, 19
why of learning, brain networks, 6
Williamson & Blackburn, 72
willingness and interest
 determining, 61–62
 importance of, 55–56
Wolff (2002), 96

Y

YISD (Ysleta Independent School District), 17–19, 21–24, 62

About the Authors

Patti Kelly Ralabate, EdD, is the author of the bestseller *Your UDL Lesson Planner: The Step-by-Step Guide for Teaching All Learners* (Paul H. Brookes, 2016) and co-author of *Culturally Responsive Design for English Learners: The UDL Approach* (with Loui Lord Nelson, CAST, 2017). Dr. Ralabate is founder and executive director of PKR Professional Learning, which works with educators who are interested in transforming their instruction and learning environments to better meet the needs of all learners. As director of implementation at CAST, Dr. Ralabate guided a multidistrict Universal Design for Learning (UDL) implementation initiative funded by the Bill & Melinda Gates Foundation that applied a systems-change lens to professional learning.

During her tenure as director of the National Center on Universal Design for Learning, she was instrumental in building access to a storehouse of resources for lesson design and UDL implementation. She was the special education policy analyst for the National Education Association and an early partner in the National UDL Task Force that successfully brought UDL into federal policy. She has nearly three decades of teaching experience as a speech-language pathologist and holds a master's degree from the University of Massachusetts and a doctorate in special education from the George Washington University in Washington, DC.

Elizabeth Berquist, EdD, brings 20 years of experience in PK-12 and higher education to her current role as director of professional learning for the Baltimore County Public School District (BCPS) where she designs and delivers professional learning for district leaders. BCPS is the 25th largest district in the US and serves more than 115,000 students.

Dr. Berquist began her career in BCPS, first as a classroom teacher and then as a central office staff member. She then spent eight years as a faculty member in the Department of Special Education at Towson University in Maryland, where she worked with pre-service and in-service educators. Her research focused on UDL, conceptual change, faculty professional development, and enhancing university-school partnerships in professional development schools. She was also responsible for the design and administration of a multiyear Universal Design for Learning Professional Development Network (UDL PDN).

Dr. Berquist won numerous teaching awards at Towson before returning to BCPS in 2015. A frequent presenter at national conferences and a member of CAST's National Faculty, she is the editor of *UDL: Moving from Exploration to Integration* (CAST, 2017), the first book to consider scaled-up implementation of UDL in schools, districts, and states.

Illustration by Eli Brophy, Philadelphia, PA

www.ingramcontent.com/pod-product-compliance
Lightning Source LLC
Chambersburg PA
CBHW081742100526
44592CB00015B/2271

In *Your UDL Journey: A Systems Approach to Transforming Instruction*, Patti Kelly Ralabate and Elizabeth Berquist draw on years of working with schools, districts, universities, and states to put the inclusive principles of Universal Design for Learning (UDL) into practice.

The authors provide a guide—not a rigid step-by-step manual—for adopting UDL as the conceptual framework for an entire system, not just individual classrooms. They clarify the difference between mere change and true transformation in a system, offering a welcome solution to the common "flavor-of-the-month" dilemma that school leaders at all levels so often face.

Your UDL Journey addresses challenges in learning design, instructional planning, professional development, resource allocation, and reflection. Written in a warm, collegial style, this book is filled with helpful signposts along the road to transformation.

Patti Kelly Ralabate, EdD, is a nationally recognized leader on effective instructional design for all learners using the Universal Design for Learning framework. She is the author of *Your UDL Lesson Planner: The Step-by-Step Guide for Teaching All Learners* and *Culturally Responsive Design for English Learners: The UDL Approach* (with Loui Lord Nelson).

Elizabeth Berquist, EdD, is Director of Professional Learning for the Baltimore County (MD) Public Schools. She also advises school districts across the United States on Universal Design for Learning. Her book *UDL: Moving from Exploration to Integration* offers a collection of case studies about UDL Implementation in systems, states, and schools.

www.castpublishing.org

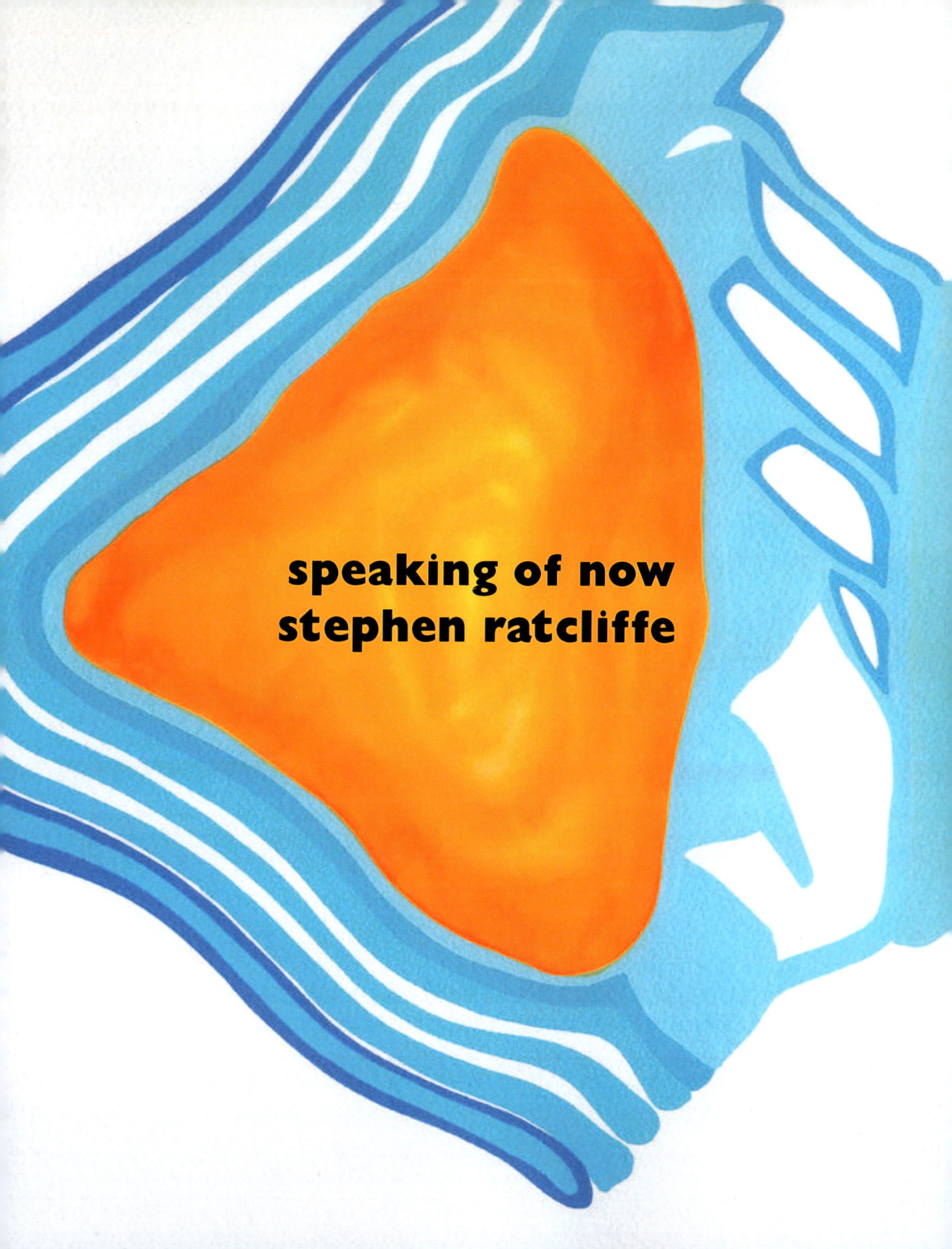